A Secure Base

Clinical applications
of attachment theory

A Secure Base

Clinical applications
of attachment theory

JOHN BOWLBY

TAVISTOCK/ROUTLEDGE
LONDON

First published in 1988
by Routledge
11 New Fetter Lane, London EC4P 4EE

Reprinted 1989

Printed in Great Britain by J. W. Arrowsmith Ltd.,
Bristol

British Library Cataloguing in Publication Data

Bowlby, John
    A secure base: clinical applications of
    attachment theory.
    1. Personality
    I. Title
155.2'5   BF698

ISBN 0-415-00640-6

To
Mary D.S. Ainsworth
who introduced the concept of
a secure base

Contents

Preface

In 1979, under the title of *The Making and Breaking of Affectional Bonds*, I published a small collection of lectures that I had given to a variety of audiences during the two preceding decades. In this volume I present a further selection of the lectures given since then. Each of the first five was delivered to a particular audience on a particular occasion; details of each are described in a brief preamble. The remaining three are extended versions of lectures given in extempore form to audiences made up of mental health professionals in countries of Europe and America. As in the earlier collection, I have thought it best to print each lecture in a form close to that in which it was originally published.

Since the theory of attachment provides the basis for every lecture some deletions have been necessary to avoid an excess of repetition. It is hoped that such as remains will, by presenting the same ideas in different contexts, clarify and emphasize distinctive features of the theory.

It is a little unexpected that, whereas attachment theory was formulated by a clinician for use in the diagnosis and treatment of emotionally disturbed patients and families, its usage hitherto has been mainly to promote research in developmental psychology. Whilst I welcome the findings of this research as enormously extending our understanding of personality development and psychopathology, and thus as of the greatest clinical relevance, it has none the less been disappointing that clinicians have been so slow to test the theory's uses. There are probably many reasons for this. One is that initially the data drawn on appeared to be unduly behavioural. Another is that clinicians are very busy people who are naturally reluctant to spend time trying to master a new and strange conceptual framework until they have strong reasons for believing that to do so will improve their clinical understanding and therapeutic skills. For those who have decided the time has come to sample what this new perspective has to offer I hope the lectures gathered here may provide a convenient introduction.

Acknowledgements

During the past ten years I have had the great benefit of frequent communication with staff and students at the Tavistock Clinic and also with a number of colleagues engaged in pioneering studies of how patterns of attachment develop during infancy and childhood. To all of them I owe a deep debt of gratitude, often for useful suggestions, sometimes for necessary corrections, and always for stimulation and encouragement. To my secretary, Dorothy Southern, I also owe a deep debt of gratitude for many years of devoted service during which she has made my interests her own.

For editorial assistance in preparing these lectures for publication and for constructing the index my thanks are due to Molly Townsend.

The first six lectures in this book have appeared in other publications and I am grateful to the publishers concerned for permission to reproduce them here. Lecture 1 was chapter 18 in *Parenthood: A Psychodynamic Perspective* edited by Rebecca S. Cohen, Bertram J. Cohler, and Sidney H. Weissman, the Guilford Press, New York (1984); Lecture 2 was 'Attachment and loss: retrospect and prospect', *American Journal of Orthopsychiatry* 52: 664–78 (1982); Lecture 3 was 'Psychoanalysis as art and science', *International Review of Psychoanalysis* 6: 3–14 (1979); Lecture 4 was 'Psychoanalysis as a natural science', *International Review of Psychoanalysis* 8: 243–56 (1981); Lecture 5 was 'Violence in the family as a disorder of the attachment and caregiving systems', *The American Journal of Psychoanalysis* 44: 9–27 (1984); Lecture 6 was chapter 6 in *Cognition and Psychotherapy* edited by Michael J. Mahoney and Arthur Freeman, Plenum Publishing Corporation, New York and London (1985), expanded from 'On knowing what you are not supposed to know and feeling what you are not supposed to feel', *Canadian Journal of Psychiatry* 24:403–8 (1979).

John Bowlby

LECTURE 1

Caring for children

During the early months of 1980 I was giving lectures in the United States. Amongst invitations reaching me was one from the psychiatric staff of the Michael Reese Hospital in Chicago to address a conference on parenting.

An indispensable social role

At some time of their lives, I believe, most human beings desire to have children and desire also that their children should grow up to be healthy, happy, and self-reliant. For those who succeed the rewards are great; but for those who have children but fail to rear them to be healthy, happy, and self-reliant the penalties in anxiety, frustration, friction, and perhaps shame or guilt, may be severe. Engaging in parenthood therefore is playing for high stakes. Furthermore, because successful parenting is a principal key to the mental health of the next generation, we need to know all we can both about its nature and about the manifold social and psychological conditions that influence its development for better or worse. The theme is a huge one and all I can do in this contribution is to sketch the approach that I myself adopt in thinking about these issues. That approach is an ethological one.

Before I go into detail, however, I want to make a few more

1

general remarks. To be a successful parent means a lot of very hard work. Looking after a baby or toddler is a twenty-four-hour-a-day job seven days a week, and often a very worrying one at that. And even if the load lightens a little as children get older, if they are to flourish they still require a lot of time and attention. For many people today these are unpalatable truths. Giving time and attention to children means sacrificing other interests and other activities. Yet I believe the evidence for what I am saying is unimpeachable. Study after study, including those pioneered in Chicago by Grinker (1962) and continued by Offer (1969), attest that healthy, happy, and self-reliant adolescents and young adults are the products of stable homes in which both parents give a great deal of time and attention to the children.

I want also to emphasize that, despite voices to the contrary, looking after babies and young children is no job for a single person. If the job is to be well done and the child's principal caregiver is not to be too exhausted, the caregiver herself (or himself) needs a great deal of assistance. From whom that help comes will vary: very often it is the other parent; in many societies, including more often than is realized our own, it comes from a grandmother. Others to be drawn in to help are adolescent girls and young women. In most societies throughout the world these facts have been, and still are, taken for granted and the society organized accordingly. Paradoxically it has taken the world's richest societies to ignore these basic facts. Man and woman power devoted to the production of material goods counts a plus in all our economic indices. Man and woman power devoted to the production of happy, healthy, and self-reliant children in their own homes does not count at all. We have created a topsy-turvy world.

But I do not want to enter into complex political and economic arguments. My reason for raising these points is to remind you that the society we live in is not only, in evolutionary terms, a product of yesterday but in many ways a very peculiar one. There is in consequence a great danger that we shall adopt mistaken norms. For, just as a society in which there is a chronic insufficiency of food may take a deplorably inadequate level of nutrition as its norm, so may a society in which parents of young children are left on their own with a chronic insufficiency of help take this state of affairs as its norm.

An ethological approach

I said earlier that my approach to an understanding of parenting as a human activity is an ethological one. Let me explain.

In re-examining the nature of the child's tie to his* mother, traditionally referred to as dependency, it has been found useful to regard it as the resultant of a distinctive and in part pre-programmed set of behaviour patterns which in the ordinary expectable environment develop during the early months of life and have the effect of keeping the child in more or less close proximity to his mother-figure (Bowlby 1969). By the end of the first year the behaviour is becoming organized cybernetically, which means, among other things, that the behaviour becomes active whenever certain conditions obtain and ceases when certain other conditons obtain. For example, a child's attachment behaviour is activated especially by pain, fatigue, and anything frightening, and also by the mother being or appearing to be inaccessible. The conditions that terminate the behaviour vary according to the intensity of its arousal. At low intensity they may be simply sight or sound of the mother, especially effective being a signal from her acknowledging his presence. At higher intensity termination may require his touching or clinging to her. At highest intensity, when he is distressed and anxious, nothing but a prolonged cuddle will do. The biological function of this behaviour is postulated to be protection, especially protection from predators.

In the example just given the individuals concerned are a child and his mother. It is evident, however, that attachment behaviour is in no way confined to children. Although usually less readily aroused, we see it also in adolescents and adults of both sexes whenever they are anxious or under stress. No one should be surprised therefore when a woman expecting a baby or

---

* Throughout this book the child is referred to as masculine in order to avoid clumsy constructions.

a mother caring for young children has a strong desire to be cared for and supported herself. The activation of attachment behaviour in these circumstances is probably universal and must be considered the norm.*

A feature of attachment behaviour of the greatest importance clinically, and present irrespective of the age of the individual concerned, is the intensity of the emotion that accompanies it, the kind of emotion aroused depending on how the relationship between the individual attached and the attachment figure is faring. If it goes well, there is joy and a sense of security. If it is threatened, there is jealousy, anxiety, and anger. If broken, there is grief and depression. Finally there is strong evidence that how attachment behaviour comes to be organized within an individual turns in high degree on the kinds of experience he has in his family of origin, or, if he is unlucky, out of it.

This type of theory I believe to have many advantages over the theories hitherto current in our field. For not only does it bring theory into close relationship with observed data but it provides a theoretical framework for the field compatible with the framework adopted throughout modern biology and neurophysiology.

Parenting, I believe, can usefully be approached from the same ethologically inspired viewpoint. This entails observing and describing the set of behaviour patterns characteristic of parenting, the conditions that activate and terminate each, how the patterns change as a child grows older, the varying ways that parenting behaviour becomes organized in different individuals and the myriad of experiences that influence how it develops in any one person.

Implicit in this approach is the assumption that parenting behaviour, like attachment behaviour, is in some degree pre-programmed and therefore ready to develop along certain lines when conditions elicit it. This means that, in the ordinary course of events, the parent of a baby experiences a strong urge to behave in certain typical sorts of way, for example, to cradle

* An increased desire for care, either from husband or mother, has been reported in studies of representative groups of women by Wenner (1966) and Ballou (1978).

the infant, to soothe him when he cries, to keep him warm, protected, and fed. Such a viewpoint, of course, does not imply that the appropriate behaviour patterns manifest themselves complete in every detail from the first. Clearly that is not so, neither in man nor in any other mammalian species. All the detail is learned, some of it during interaction with babies and children, much of it through observation of how other parents behave, starting during the parent-to-be's own childhood and the way his parents treated him and his siblings.

This modern view of behavioural development contrasts sharply with both of the older paradigms, one of which, invoking instinct, over-emphasized the preprogrammed component and the other of which, reacting against instinct, overemphasized the learned component. Parenting behaviour in humans is certainly not the product of some unvarying parenting instinct, but nor is it reasonable to regard it as the product simply of learning. Parenting behaviour, as I see it, has strong biological roots, which accounts for the very strong emotions associated with it; but the detailed form that the behaviour takes in each of us turns on our experiences – experiences during childhood especially, experiences during adolescence, experiences before and during marriage, and experiences with each individual child.

Thus I regard it as useful to look upon parenting behaviour as one example of a limited class of biologically rooted types of behaviour of which attachment behaviour is another example, sexual behaviour another, and exploratory behaviour and eating behaviour yet others. Each of these types of behaviour contributes in its own specific way to the survival either of the individual or his offspring. It is indeed because each one serves so vital a function that each of these types of behaviour is in some degree preprogrammed. To leave their development solely to the caprices of individual learning would be the height of biological folly.

You will notice that in sketching this framework I am making a point of keeping each of these types of behaviour conceptually distinct from the others. This contrasts, of course, with traditional libido theory which has treated them as the varying expressions of a single drive. The reasons for keeping them

5

distinct are several. One is that each of the types of behaviour mentioned serves its own distinctive biological function – protection, reproduction, nutrition, knowledge of the environment. Another is that many of the detailed patterns of behaviour within each general type are distinctive also: clinging to a parent is different from soothing and comforting a child; sucking or chewing food is different from engaging in sexual intercourse. Furthermore, factors which influence the development of one of these types of behaviour are not necessarily the same as those that influence the development of another. By keeping them distinct we are able to study not only the ways in which they differ but also the ways in which they overlap and interact with each other – as it has long been evident they do.

Initiation of mother–infant interaction

During the past decade or so there has been a dramatic advance in our understanding of the early phases of mother–infant interaction, thanks to the imaginative research of workers on both sides of the Atlantic. The studies of Klaus and Kennell are now well known. Of special interest here are their observations of how mothers behave towards their newborns when given freedom to do what they like after delivery. Klaus, Trause, and Kennell (1975) describe how a mother, immediately after her infant is born, picks him up and begins to stroke his face with her finger tips. At this the baby quietens. Soon she moves on to touching his head and body with the palm of her hand and, within five or six minutes, she is likely to put him to her breast. The baby responds with prolonged licking of the nipple. 'Immediately after the delivery', they noted, 'the mothers appeared to be in a state of ecstasy', and, interestingly enough, the observers became elated too. From the moment of birth attention becomes riveted on the baby. Something about him tends to draw not only the mother and father but all those present to the new arrival. Given the chance, a mother is likely during the next few days to spend many hours just looking at her new possession, cuddling him, and getting to know him. Usually there comes a moment when she feels the baby is her very own. For some it comes early; perhaps when she first holds him or when he first looks into her eyes. For a large minority of primaparae who are delivered in hospital, however, it may be delayed for up to a week, often until they are home again (Robson and Kumar 1980).

Phenomena of the greatest importance to which recent research has drawn attention are the potential of the healthy neonate to enter into an elemental form of social interaction and the potential of the ordinary sensitive mother to participate successfully in it.*

When a mother and her infant of two or three weeks are facing one another, phases of lively social interaction occur, alternating with phases of disengagement. Each phase of interaction begins with initiation and mutual greeting, builds up to an animated interchange comprising facial expressions and vocalizations, during which the infant orients towards his mother with excited movements of arms and legs; then his activities gradually subside and end with the baby looking away for a spell before the next phase of interaction begins. Throughout these cycles the baby is likely to be as spontaneously active as his mother. Where their roles differ is in the timing of their responses. Whereas an infant's initiation and withdrawal from interaction tend to follow his own autonomous rhythm, a sensitive mother regulates her behaviour so that it meshes with his. In addition she modifies the form her behaviour takes to suit him: her voice is gentle but higher pitched than usual, her movements slowed, and each next action adjusted in form and timing according to how her baby is performing. Thus she lets him call the tune and by a skilful interweaving of her own responses with his creates a dialogue.

The speed and efficiency with which these dialogues develop and the mutual enjoyment they give point clearly to each participant being preadapted to engage in them. On the one hand is

---

* See especially the work of Stern (1977), Sander (1977), Brazelton, Koslowski, and Main (1974) and Schaffer (1977). For excellent reviews see Schaffer (1979) and Stern (1985). The state of heightened sensitivity that develops in a woman during and especially towards the end of pregnancy, and that enables her 'to adapt delicately and sensitively' to her infant's needs, is a process to which Winnicott (1957) has called attention.

7

the mother's intuitive readiness to allow her interventions to be paced by her infant. On the other is the readiness with which the infant's rhythms shift gradually to take account of the timing of his mother's interventions. In a happily developing partnership each is adapting to the other.

Very similar alternating sequences have been recorded in other quite different exchanges between mother and child. For example, Kaye (1977), observing the behaviour of mother and infant during feeding, has found that mothers tend to interact with their infants in precise synchrony with the infant's pattern of sucking and pausing. During bursts of sucking a mother is generally quiet and inactive; during pauses she strokes and talks to her baby. Another example of mother taking her cue from her infant, in this case an infant within the age range 5 to 12 months, is reported by Collis and Schaffer (1975). A mother and her infant are introduced to a scene in which there are a number of large brightly coloured toys which quickly seize their visual attention. Observation of their behaviour then shows two things. First, both partners as a rule are looking at the same object at the same time. Secondly, examination of the timing shows almost invariably that it is the baby who leads and the mother who follows. The baby's spontaneous interest in the toys is evidently closely monitored by his mother who almost automatically then looks in the same direction. A focus of mutual interest having been established, mother is likely to elaborate on it, commenting on the toy, naming it, manipulating it. 'A sharing experience is then brought about, instigated by the infant's spontaneous attention to the environment but established by the mother allowing herself to be paced by the baby'.

Yet another example, also reported by Schaffer (Schaffer, Collis, and Parsons 1977), concerns vocal interchange between mother and child at a preverbal level. In a comparison of two groups of children, aged 12 and 24 months, it was found that the ability of the pair to take turns and to avoid overlapping was not only strikingly efficient but as characteristic of the younger as of the older infants. Thus, long before the appearance of words, the pattern of turn-taking so characteristic of human conversation is already present. Here again the evidence suggests that, in ensuring the smooth transitions from one 'speaker' to the other, mother is playing the major part.

My reason for giving these examples at some length is that I believe they illustrate some basic principles both about parenting and about the nature of the creature who is parented. What emerges from these studies is that the ordinary sensitive mother is quickly attuned to her infant's natural rhythms and, by attending to the details of his behaviour, discovers what suits him and behaves accordingly. By so doing she not only makes him contented but also enlists his co-operation. For, although initially his capacity to adapt is limited, it is not absent altogether and, if allowed to grow in its own time, is soon yielding rewards. Ainsworth and her colleagues have noted that infants whose mothers have responded sensitively to their signals during the first year of life not only cry less during the second half of that year than do the babies of less responsive mothers but are more willing to fall in with their parent's wishes (Ainsworth *et al.* 1978). Human infants, we can safely conclude, like infants of other species, are preprogrammed to develop in a socially co-operative way; whether they do so or not turns in high degree on how they are treated.

This is a view of human nature, you will notice, radically different from the one that has long been current in western societies and that has permeated so much of the clinical theory and practice we have inherited. It points, of course, to a radically different conception of the role of parent.

Roles of mothers and fathers: similarities and differences

In the examples given so far, the parent concerned has been the mother. This is almost inevitable because for research purposes it is relatively easy to recruit samples of infants who are being cared for mainly by their mother, whereas infants being cared for mainly by their father are comparatively scarce. Let me therefore describe briefly one of several recent studies which, together, go some way to correct the balance.

Several hundred infants have now been studied by means of the strange situation procedure devised by Ainsworth (Ainsworth *et al.* 1978) which gives an opportunity to observe how the infant responds, first in his parent's presence, next when he is left alone, and later when his parent returns. As a result of these observations infants can be classified as presenting a pattern either of secure attachment to mother or of one of two main forms of insecure attachment to her. Since these patterns have been shown to have considerable stability during the earliest years of life and to predict how a nursery-school child in the age range $4\frac{1}{2}$ to 6 years will approach a new person and tackle a new task (Arend, Gove, and Sroufe 1979), the value of the procedure as a method of assessing an infant's social and emotional development needs no emphasis.

Hitherto almost all the studies using this procedure have observed infants with their mothers. Main and Weston (1981), however, extended the work by observing some sixty infants, first with one parent and, six months later, with the other. One finding was that, when looked at as a group, the patterns of attachment that were shown to fathers resembled closely the patterns that were shown to mothers, with roughly the same percentage distribution of patterns. But a second finding was even more interesting. When the patterns shown by each child individually were examined, no correlation was found between the pattern shown with one parent and the pattern shown with the other. Thus one child may have a secure relationship with the mother but not with the father, a second may have it with the father but not with the mother, a third may have it with both parents, and a fourth may have it with neither. In their approach to new people and new tasks the children represented a graded series. Children with a secure relationship to both parents were most confident and most competent; children who had a secure relationship to neither were least so; and those with a secure relationship to one parent but not to the other came in between.

Since there is evidence that the pattern of attachment a child undamaged at birth develops with his mother is the product of how his mother has treated him (Ainsworth *et al.* 1978), it is more than likely that, in a similar way, the pattern he develops with his father is the product of how his father has treated him.

This study, together with others, suggests that, by providing an attachment figure for his child, a father may be filling a role closely resembling that filled by a mother; though in most, perhaps all, cultures fathers fill that role much less frequently than do mothers, at least when the children are still young. In most families with young children the father's role is a different one. He is more likely to engage in physically active and novel play than the mother and, especially for boys, to become his child's preferred play companion.*

Provision of a secure base

This brings me to a central feature of my concept of parenting – the provision by both parents of a secure base from which a child or an adolescent can make sorties into the outside world and to which he can return knowing for sure that he will be welcomed when he gets there, nourished physically and emotionally, comforted if distressed, reassured if frightened. In essence this role is one of being available, ready to respond when called upon to encourage and perhaps assist, but to intervene actively only when clearly necessary. In these respects it is a role similar to that of the officer commanding a military base from which an expeditionary force sets out and to which it can retreat, should it meet with a setback. Much of the time the role of the base is a waiting one but it is none the less vital for that. For it is only when the officer commanding the expeditionary force is confident his base is secure that he dare press forward and take risks.

In the case of children and adolescents we see them, as they get older, venturing steadily further from base and for increasing spans of time. The more confident they are that their base is secure and, moreover, ready if called upon to respond, the more they take it for granted. Yet should one or other parent become ill or die, the immense significance of the base to the emotional equilibrium of the child or adolescent or young adult is at once apparent. In the lectures to follow evidence is presented from

* Studies of relevance are those of Lamb (1977), Parke (1979), Clarke-Stewart (1978), and Mackey (1979).

studies of adolescents and young adults, as well as of school children of different ages from nursery school up, that those who are most stable emotionally and making the most of their opportunities are those who have parents who, whilst always encouraging their children's autonomy, are none the less available and responsive when called upon. Unfortunately, of course, the reverse is also true.

No parent is going to provide a secure base for his growing child unless he has an intuitive understanding of and respect for his child's attachment behaviour and treats it as the intrinsic and valuable part of human nature I believe it to be. This is where the traditional term 'dependence' has had so baleful an influence. Dependency always carries with it an adverse valuation and tends to be regarded as a characteristic only of the early years and one which ought soon to be grown out of. As a result in clinical circles it has often happened that, whenever attachment behaviour is manifested during later years, it has not only been regarded as regrettable but has even been dubbed regressive. I believe that to be an appalling misjudgement.

In discussing parenting I have focused on the parents' role of providing a child with a secure base because, although well recognized intuitively, it has hitherto, I believe, been inadequately conceptualized. But there are, of course, many other roles a parent has to play. One concerns the part a parent plays in influencing his child's behaviour in one direction or another and the range of techniques he uses to do so. Although some of these techniques are necessarily restrictive, and certain others have a disciplinary intent, many of them are of an encouraging sort, for example, calling a child's attention to a toy or some other feature of the environment, or giving him tips on how to solve a problem he cannot quite manage on his own. Plainly the repertoire of techniques used varies enormously from parent to parent – from largely helpful and encouraging to largely restrictive and punitive. An interesting start in exploring the range of techniques used by the parents of toddlers in Scotland has been made by Schaffer and Crook (1979).

Peri- and post-natal conditions that help or hinder

So far in this lecture my aim has been to describe some of the ways in which the parents of children who thrive socially and emotionally are observed to behave towards them. Fortunately, much of this behaviour comes naturally to many mothers and fathers who find the resulting interchanges with their children enjoyable and rewarding. Yet it is evident that, even when social and economic conditions are favourable, these mutually satisfying relationships do not develop in every family. Let us consider therefore what we know of the psychological conditions that foster their doing so and those that impede them.

At several points I have referred to the ordinary sensitive mother who is attuned to her child's actions and signals, who responds to them more or less appropriately, and who is then able to monitor the effects her behaviour has on her child and to modify it accordingly. The same description, no doubt, would apply to the ordinary sensitive father. Now it is clear that, in order for a parent to behave in these ways, adequate time and a relaxed atmosphere are necessary. This is where a parent, especially the mother who usually bears the brunt of parenting during the early months or years, needs all the help she can get – not in looking after her baby, which is her job, but in all the household chores.

A friend of mine, a social anthropologist, observed that in the South Sea island in which she was working it was the custom for a mother-to-be, both during and after the baby was born, to be attended by a couple of female relatives who cared for her throughout the first month, leaving her free to care for her baby. So impressed was my friend by these humane arrangements that, when her own baby was born on the island, she accepted suggestions that she be cared for in the VIP way, and she had no cause to regret it. In addition to practical help, a congenial female companion is likely to provide the new mother with emotional support or, in my terminology, to provide for her the kind of secure base we all need in conditons of stress and without which it is difficult to relax. In almost all societies an arrangement of this sort is the rule. Indeed in all but one of 150 cultures studied by anthropologists a family member or friend, usually a woman, remains with a mother throughout labour and delivery (Raphael 1966, quoted by Sosa *et al.* 1980).

Turning to our own society, preliminary findings that, if confirmed, are of the greatest interest and practical importance have recently been reported by the Klaus and Kennell team from a study conducted in a hospital maternity unit in Guatemala (Sosa *et al.* 1980). One group of women went through labour and delivery according to the routine practice of the unit which meant in effect that the woman was left alone for most of the time. The other group received constant friendly support from an untrained lay woman from the time of admission until delivery, one woman during the day and another at night. In the supported group labour was less than half as long as in the other, 8.7 hours against 19.3.* Moreover, the mother was awake for a greater part of the first hour of the infant's life during which she was much more likely to be seen stroking her baby, smiling, and talking to him.

Effects of a similar kind on the way a mother treats her baby as a result of her having additional contact with him soon after his birth are now well known. Amongst differences observed by Klaus and Kennell, when the babies were one month old, was that a mother given extra contact was more likely to comfort her baby during stressful clinic visits and, during feeding, was more likely to fondle the baby and engage him in eye-to-eye contact. Differences of a comparable kind were observed when the babies were 12 months old and again at 2 years. In these studies the increased contact amounted to no more than an extra hour within the first three hours after birth, with a further five of contact each afternoon during the next three days (Kennell *et al.* 1974; Ringler *et al.* 1975).†

* In a further and larger study, also carried out in Guatemala and by the same research group, all findings were replicated. Samples numbered 279 in the routine group and 186 in the supported group. Not only was the duration of labour halved but the incidence of perinatal complications halved also (Klaus *et al.* 1986).

† Since more recent studies, e.g. Svejda, Campos, and Emde (1980), have failed to replicate initial findings of the effects of early mother–infant contact, the issue remains in doubt. It may be that in this sensitive area details of how this early contact is arranged and by whom would explain discrepancies.

Findings of another study of the part these kinds of peri- and post-natal experiences play in either assisting a mother to develop a loving and sensitive relationship to her baby or impeding it are reported by Peterson and Mehl (1978). In a longitudinal study of forty-six women and their husbands, interviewed and observed during pregnancy, labour, and on four occasions during the infants' first six months, the most significant variable predicting differences in maternal bonding was the length of time a mother had been separated from her baby during the hours and days after his birth. Other variables that played a significant but lesser part were the birth experience and the attitudes and expectations expressed by the mother during her pregnancy.

Influence of parents' childhood experiences

There is, of course, much clinical evidence that a mother's feeling for and behaviour towards her baby are deeply influenced also by her previous personal experiences, especially those she has had and may still be having with her own parents; and, though the evidence of this in regard to a father's attitudes is less plentiful, what there is points clearly to the same conclusion.

On this matter evidence from systematic studies of young children is impressive: it shows that the influence that parents have on the pattern of caring that their children develop starts very early. For example, Zahn-Waxler, Radke-Yarrow, and King (1979) have found not only that aiding and comforting others in distress is a pattern of behaviour that commonly develops as early as a child's second year of life, but that the form it takes is much influenced by how a mother treats her child. Children whose mothers respond sensitively to their signals and provide comforting bodily contact are those who respond most readily and appropriately to the distress of others.* Not infrequently, moreover, what a child does in such circumstances is a clear

---

* The role of close physical contact with mother during human infancy has been studied especially by Ainsworth who finds that children who develop a secure attachment to mother are those who, during early infancy, are held longest in a tender and loving way (Ainsworth *et al.* 1978).

15

replica of what he has seen and/or experienced his mother do. The follow-up of a group of children showing these early differences would be of the greatest interest.

Another line of evidence regarding the influence of childhood experience on how a woman mothers her child comes from studies undertaken in London. For example, a study by Frommer and O'Shea (1973) shows that women who, during their pregnancy, give a history of having been separated from one or both parents before the age of 11 years are particularly likely to have marital and psychological difficulties after their baby's birth and also to have trouble with their infants' feeding and sleeping. Another study, also in London, by Wolkind, Hall, and Pawlby (1977) is extending this finding by showing that women with this type of childhood history interact significantly less with their 5-month-old first-born infants than do women who have had more settled childhoods. These observations, which were carried out by an ethologist, extended over a period long enough to record fifty minutes of the baby's waking life, exclusive of any time taken to feed him; this usually necessitated the observer staying for the whole morning. Not only did the mothers from a disrupted family of origin spend on average twice as long as the other mothers out of sight of their babies, but, even when one of them was with her baby, she was likely to spend less time holding him, less time looking at him and less time talking to him. Moreover, when asked the question, 'It takes a bit of time to begin to see a baby as a person - do you feel this yet?', mothers from a disrupted family were much less likely to say they did (Hall, Pawlby, and Wolkind 1979). The point I wish to emphasize is that the study provides firm evidence that women whose childhood has been disturbed tend to engage in less interaction with their infants than do mothers with happier childhoods – at a period in their baby's life when the amount of interaction that ensues is determined almost entirely by the mother.

Some of the clearest evidence regarding the enormous part played by childhood experience in determining in later years how a parent treats a child comes from studies of parents known to have abused their children physically (Parke and Collmer 1979). A common picture includes a childhood in which parental care was at best erratic and at worst absent altogether, in which criticism and blame were frequent and bitter, and in which parents or step-parents had behaved violently towards each other and sometimes though not always towards the children. A feature that emerges from a study by DeLozier of mothers known to have abused a child physically (a study described in detail in Lecture 5) is the high proportion who have lived in constant dread of being deserted by one or both parents and therefore of being sent away to foster home or institution, and who have also been threatened frequently with violent beatings or worse. Not surprisingly these girls have grown up to be perpetually anxious lest husband or boy-friend desert, to regard physical violence as part of the natural order, and to expect little or nothing in the way of love or support from any quarter.

Not every woman with childhood experiences of these sorts batters her child, however; nor indeed does a woman who physically abuses one of her children necessarily abuse the others. What accounts for these differences? Evidence suggests that individuals who, thanks to earlier experiences, are markedly prone to develop unfavourable parental attitudes are more than usually sensitive to what happens to them in the time during and after the birth of their babies. It seems that for these women adverse experiences during this time can prove the last straw.

In a study done at Oxford, for example, Lynch (1975) compared the histories of twenty-five children who had been physically abused with those of their siblings who had escaped. Children who had been abused were significantly more likely than their siblings to have been the product of an abnormal pregnancy, labour, or delivery, to have been separated from their mother for forty-eight hours or more soon after birth, and to have experienced separations of other kinds during their first six months of life. During the first year of these children's lives, moreover, the abused children were much more likely to have been ill than were the non-abused siblings; and the mothers also were more likely to have been ill during the abused child's first year than during the siblings' first year. Since in this study the personalities and childhood histories of the parents were the same for the abused siblings as for the non-abused, the fate of each seems to have turned in large part on the mother's

17

experiences with the child during the peri- and early post-natal periods. The findings of a study by Cater and Easton (1980) point to the same conclusion.*

Of the many other disturbed patterns of parenting that can be traced, in part at least, to childhood experience, there is one that happens also to be well documented in studies of abusing mothers (e.g. Morris and Gould 1963; Steele and Pollock 1968; Green, Gaines, and Sandgrun 1974; DeLozier 1982). This is their tendency to expect and demand care and attention from their own children, in other words to invert the relationship. During interview they regularly describe how, as children, they too had been made to feel responsible for looking after their parents instead of the parents caring for them.

Most, perhaps all, parents who expect their children to care for them have experienced very inadequate parenting themselves. Unfortunately, all too often, they then create major psychological problems for their children. Elsewhere (Bowlby 1973, 1980) I have argued that an inverted parent–child relationship of this kind lies behind a significant proportion of cases of school refusal (school phobia) and agoraphobia, and also probably of depression.

How we can best help

In this contribution I have given principal attention to what we know about successful parenting and to some of the variables that make it easier or more difficult for young men and women to become sensitive, caring parents. In consequence I have been able to say only a little about the many and varied patterns of deficient and distorted parenting that we meet with clinically. Another large theme omitted is how we can best help young men and women become the successful parents I believe the great majority wish to be. In conclusion, therefore, let me state what I believe to be the first principles for such work – which are

---

* In interpreting the findings of these two studies caution is necessary because in neither study is it certain that in every case the child's mother was always the abusing parent.

that we seek always to teach by example, not precept, by discussion, not instruction. The more that we can give young people opportunities to meet with and observe *at first hand* how sensitive, caring parents treat their offspring, the more likely are they to follow suit. To learn directly from such parents about the difficulties they meet with and the rewards they obtain, and to discuss with them both their mistakes and their successes, are worth, I believe, hundreds of instructional talks. For a programme of this kind, which in some places might be an extension of the mothers' self-help groups now beginning to flourish, we would need to enlist the active co-operation of sensitive, caring parents. Fortunately there are still plenty of them in our society and I believe many would be willing and proud to help.

LECTURE 2

The origins of attachment theory

In the spring of 1981 the American Orthopsychiatric Association invited me to New York to receive the Fourth Blanche Ittleson Award and to address members of the Association on the history of my work in the field of attachment and loss. After thanking members for the honour they were doing me, I also took the opportunity to express my deep gratitude to the three American foundations, the Josiah Macy Junior, the Ford, and the Foundations Fund for Research in Psychiatry, which had supported our work at the Tavistock Clinic during the critical decade starting in 1953.

After the meeting the editor of the Association's journal asked me to expand my remarks by giving an account of what we knew at that time in the field I have been exploring, how we arrived at that knowledge, and the directions which further research should take. In reply I explained that I was in no position to be an objective historian in a field that had for long been controversial and that all I could attempt was to describe the story as I recalled it and to point to a few of the empirical studies and theoretical ideas that had been influential in shaping it. My personal biases, I explained, would inevitably be everywhere evident.

During the nineteen-thirties and forties a number of clinicians on both sides of the Atlantic, mostly working independently of each other, were making observations of the ill effects on personality development of prolonged institutional care and/or

20

frequent changes of mother-figure during the early years of life. Influential publications followed. Listing authors in alphabetical order of surname, these include the following: Lauretta Bender (Bender and Yarnell 1941, Bender 1947), John Bowlby (1940, 1944), Dorothy Burlingham and Anna Freud (1942, 1944), William Goldfarb (1943 a, b, and c and six other papers, summarized 1955), David Levy (1937), and René Spitz (1945, 1946). Since each of the authors was a qualified analyst (except for Goldfarb who trained later), it is no surprise that the findings created little stir outside analytical circles.

At that point, late 1949, an imaginative young British psychiatrist, analytically oriented and recently appointed to be Chief of the Mental Health Section of the World Health Organisation, stepped in. Requested to contribute to a United Nations study of the needs of homeless children, Ronald Hargreaves* decided to appoint a short-term consultant to report on the mental health aspects of the problem and, knowing of my interest in the field, invited me to undertake the task. For me this was a golden opportunity. After five years as an army psychiatrist, I had returned to child psychiatry determined to explore further the problems I had begun working on before the war; and I had already appointed as my first research assistant James Robertson, a newly qualified psychiatric social worker who had worked with Anna Freud in the Hampstead Nurseries during the war.

The six months I spent with the World Health Organisation in 1950 gave me the chance not only to read the literature and to discuss it with the authors, but also to meet many others in Europe and the United States with experience of the field. Soon after the end of my contract I submitted my report, which was published early in 1951 as a WHO monograph entitled *Maternal Care and Mental Health*. In it I reviewed the far from negligible evidence then available regarding the adverse influences on personality development of inadequate maternal care during early childhood, called attention to the acute distress of young children who find themselves separated from those they know

* Ronald Hargreaves's premature death in 1962, when professor of psychiatry at Leeds, was a grievous loss to preventive psychiatry.

and love, and made recommendations of how best to avoid, or at least mitigate, the short- and long-term ill effects. During the next few years this report was translated into a dozen other languages and appeared also in a cheap abridged edition in English.

Influential though the written word may often be, it has nothing like the emotional impact of a movie. Throughout the nineteen-fifties René Spitz's early film *Grief: A Peril in Infancy* (1947), and James Robertson's *A Two-Year-Old Goes to Hospital* (1952) together had an enormous influence. Not only did they draw the attention of professional workers to the immediate distress and anxiety of young children in an institutional setting but they proved powerful instruments for promoting changes in practice. In this field Robertson was to play a leading part (e.g. Robertson 1958, 1970).

Although by the end of the nineteen-fifties a great many of those working in child psychiatry and psychology and in social work, and some also of those in paediatrics and sick children's nursing, had accepted the research findings and were implementing change, the sharp controversy aroused by the early publications and films continued. Psychiatrists trained in traditional psychiatry and psychologists who adopted a learning-theory approach never ceased to point to the deficiencies of the evidence and to the lack of an adequate explanation of how the types of experience implicated could have the effects on personality development claimed. Many psychoanalysts, in addition, especially those whose theory focused on the role of fantasy in psychopathology to the relative exclusion of the influence of real life events, remained unconvinced and sometimes very critical. Meanwhile, research continued. For example, at Yale Sally Provence and Rose Lipton were making a systematic study of institutionalized infants in which they compared their development with that of infants living in a family (Provence and Lipton 1962). At the Tavistock members of my small research group were active collecting further data on the short-term effects on a young child of being in the care of strange people in a strange place for weeks and sometimes months at a time (see especially the studies by Christoph Heinicke (1956) and, with Ilse Westheimer, (1966)),

22

whilst I addressed myself to the theoretical problems posed by our data.

Meanwhile the field was changing. One important influence was the publication in 1963 by the World Health Organisation of a collection of articles in which the manifold effects of the various types of experience covered by the term 'deprivation of maternal care' were reassessed. Of the six articles, by far the most comprehensive was by my colleague Mary Ainsworth (1962). In it she not only reviewed the extensive and diverse evidence and considered the many issues that had given rise to controversy but also identified a large number of problems requiring further research.

A second important influence was the publication, beginning during the late fifties, of Harry Harlow's studies of the effects of maternal deprivation on rhesus monkeys; and once again film played a big part. Harlow's work in the United States had been stimulated by Spitz's reports. In the United Kingdom complementary studies by Robert Hinde had been stimulated by our work at the Tavistock. For the next decade a stream of experimental results from those two scientists (see summaries in Harlow and Harlow 1965 and Hinde and Spencer-Booth 1971), coming on top of the Ainsworth review, undermined the opposition. Thereafter nothing more was heard of the inherent implausibility of our hypotheses; and criticism became more constructive.

Much, of course, remained uncertain. Even if the reality of short-term distress and behavioural disturbance is granted, what evidence is there, it was asked, that the ill effects can persist? What features of the experience, or combination of features, are responsible for the distress? And, should it prove true that in some cases ill effects do persist, how is that to be accounted for? How does it happen that some children seem to come through very unfavourable experiences relatively unharmed? How important is it that a child should be cared for most of the time by one principal caregiver? In less developed societies it was claimed (wrongly as it turns out) that multiple mothering is not uncommon. In addition to all these legitimate questions, moreover, there were misunderstandings. Some supposed that advocates of the view that a child should be cared for most of the time by a principal mother-figure held that that had to be the child's natural mother – the so-called blood-tie theory. Others supposed that, in advocating that a child should 'experience a warm intimate and continuous relationship with his mother (or permanent mother-substitute)', proponents were prescribing a regime in which a mother had to care for her child twenty-four hours a day, day in and day out, with no respite. In a field in which strong feelings are aroused and almost everyone has some sort of vested interest, clear unbiased thinking is not always easy.

A new look at theory

The monograph *Maternal Care and Mental Health* is in two parts. The first reviews the evidence regarding the adverse effects of maternal deprivation, the second discusses means for preventing it. What was missing, as several reviewers pointed out, was any explanation of how experiences subsumed under the broad heading of maternal deprivation could have the effects on personality development of the kinds claimed. The reason for this omission was simple: the data were not accommodated by any theory then current and in the brief time of my employment by the World Health Organisation there was no possibility of developing a new one.

The child's tie to his mother

At that time it was widely held that the reason a child develops a close tie to his mother is that she feeds him. Two kinds of drive are postulated, primary and secondary. Food is thought of as primary; the personal relationship, referred to as 'dependency', as secondary. This theory did not seem to me to fit the facts. For example, were it true, an infant of a year or two should take readily to whomever feeds him and this clearly was not the case. An alternative theory, stemming from the Hungarian school of psychoanalysis, postulated a primitive object relation from the beginning. In its best-known version, however, the one advocated by Melanie Klein, mother's breast is postulated as the

24

first object, and the greatest emphasis is placed on food and orality and on the infantile nature of 'dependency'. None of these features matched my experience of children.

But if the current dependency theories were inadequate, what was the alternative?

During the summer of 1951 a friend mentioned to me the work of Lorenz on the following responses of ducklings and goslings. Reading about this and related work on instinctive behaviour revealed a new world, one in which scientists of high calibre were investigating in non-human species many of the problems with which we were grappling in the human, in particular the relatively enduring relationships that develop in many species, first between young and parents and later between mated pairs, and some of the ways in which these developments can go awry. Could this work, I asked myself, cast light on a problem central to psychoanalysis, that of 'instinct' in humans?

Next followed a long phase during which I set about trying to master basic principles and to apply them to our problems, starting with the nature of the child's tie to his mother. Here Lorenz's work on the following response of ducklings and goslings (Lorenz 1935) was of special interest. It showed that in some animal species a strong bond to an individual mother-figure could develop without the intermediary of food: for these young birds *are not fed by parents* but feed themselves by catching insects. Here then was an alternative model to the traditional one, and one that had a number of features that seemed possibly to fit the human case. Thereafter, as my grasp of ethological principles increased and I applied them to one clinical problem after another, I became increasingly confident that this was a promising approach. Thus, having adopted this novel point of view, I decided to 'follow it up through the material as long as the application of it seems to yield results' (to borrow a phrase of Freud's).

From 1957, when *The Nature of the Child's Tie to his Mother* was first presented, through 1969 when *Attachment* appeared, until 1980 with the publication of *Loss* I concentrated on this task. The resulting conceptual framework* is designed to accommodate all

* This is the term Thomas Kuhn (1974) now uses to replace 'paradigm', the term he used in his earlier work (Kuhn 1962).

those phenomena to which Freud called attention – for example love relations, separation anxiety, mourning, defence, anger, guilt, depression, trauma, emotional detachment, sensitive periods in early life – and so to offer an alternative to the traditional metapsychology of psychoanalysis and to add yet another to the many variants of the clinical theory now extant. How successful these ideals will prove only time will tell.

As Kuhn has emphasized, any novel conceptual framework is difficult to grasp, especially so for those long familiar with a previous one. Of the many difficulties met with in understanding the framework advocated, I describe only a few. One is that, instead of starting with a clinical syndrome of later years and trying to trace its origins retrospectively, I have started with a class of childhood traumata and tried to trace the sequelae prospectively. A second is that, instead of starting with the private thoughts and feelings of a patient, as expressed in free associations or play, and trying to build a theory of personality development from those data, I have started with observations of the behaviour of children in certain sorts of defined situation, including records of the feelings and thoughts they express, and have tried to build a theory of personality development from there. Other difficulties arise from my use of concepts such as control system (instead of psychic energy) and developmental pathway (instead of libidinal phase), which, although now firmly established as key concepts in all the biological sciences, are still foreign to the thinking of a great many psychologists and clinicians.

Having discarded the secondary-drive, dependency theory of the child's tie to his mother, and also the Kleinian alternative, a first task was to formulate a replacement. This led to the concept of attachment behaviour with its own dynamics distinct from the behaviour and dynamics of either feeding or sex, the two sources of human motivation for long widely regarded as the most fundamental. Strong support for this step soon came from Harlow's finding that, in another primate species – rhesus macaques – infants show a marked preference for a soft dummy 'mother', despite its providing no food, to a hard one that does provide it (Harlow and Zimmermann 1959).

Attachment behaviour is any form of behaviour that results

in a person attaining or maintaining proximity to some other clearly identified individual who is conceived as better able to cope with the world. It is most obvious whenever the person is frightened, fatigued, or sick, and is assuaged by comforting and caregiving. At other times the behaviour is less in evidence. Nevertheless for a person to know that an attachment figure is available and responsive gives him a strong and pervasive feeling of security, and so encourages him to value and continue the relationship. Whilst attachment behaviour is at its most obvious in early childhood, it can be observed throughout the life cycle, especially in emergencies. Since it is seen in virtually all human beings (though in varying patterns), it is regarded as an integral part of human nature and one we share (to a varying extent) with members of other species. The biological function attributed to it is that of protection. To remain within easy access of a familiar individual known to be ready and willing to come to our aid in an emergency is clearly a good insurance policy – whatever our age.

By conceptualizing attachment in this way, as a fundamental form of behaviour with its own internal motivation distinct from feeding and sex, and of no less importance for survival, the behaviour and motivation are accorded a theoretical status never before given them – though parents and clinicians alike have long been intuitively aware of their importance. As already emphasized, the terms 'dependency' and 'dependency need' that have hitherto been used to refer to them have serious disadvantages. In the first place 'dependency' has a perjorative flavour; in the second it does not imply an emotionally charged relationship to one or a very few clearly preferred individuals; and in the third no valuable biological function has ever been attributed to it.

It is now thirty years since the notion of attachment was first advanced as a useful way of conceptualizing a form of behaviour of central importance not only to clinicians and to developmental psychologists but to every parent as well. During that time attachment theory has been greatly clarified and amplified. The most notable contributors have been Robert Hinde who, in addition to his own publications (e.g. 1974), has constantly guided my own thinking, and Mary Ainsworth who, starting in the late fifties, has pioneered empirical studies of attachment behaviour both in Africa (1963, 1967) and in the USA (Ainsworth and Wittig 1969; Ainsworth *et al.* 1978), and has also helped greatly to develop theory (e.g. 1969, 1982). Her work, together with that of her students and others influenced by her (which has expanded dramatically since this lecture was given and is described in some detail in Lecture 7), has led attachment theory to be widely regarded as probably the best supported theory of socio-emotional development yet available (Rajecki, Lamb, and Obmascher 1978; Rutter 1980; Parkes and Stevenson-Hinde 1982; Sroufe 1986).

Because my starting point in developing theory was observations of behaviour, some clinicians have assumed that the theory amounts to no more than a version of behaviourism. This mistake is due in large part to the unfamiliarity of the conceptual framework proposed and in part to my own failure in early formulations to make clear the distinction to be drawn between an attachment and attachment behaviour. To say of a child (or older person) that he is attached to, or has an attachment to, someone means that he is strongly disposed to seek proximity to and contact with that individual and to do so especially in certain specified conditions. The disposition to behave in this way is an attribute of the attached person, a persisting attribute which changes only slowly over time and which is unaffected by the situation of the moment. Attachment behaviour, by contrast, refers to any of the various forms of behaviour that the person engages in from time to time to obtain and/or maintain a desired proximity.

There is abundant evidence that almost every child habitually prefers one person, usually his mother-figure, to whom to go when distressed but that, in her absence, he will make do with someone else, preferably someone whom he knows well. On these occasions most children show a clear hierarchy of preference so that, in extremity and with no one else available, even a kindly stranger may be approached. Thus, whilst attachment behaviour may in differing circumstances be shown to a variety of individuals, an enduring attachment, or attachment bond, is confined to very few. Should a child fail to show such clear discrimination, it is likely he is severely disturbed.

The theory of attachment is an attempt to explain both attachment behaviour, with its episodic appearance and disappearance, and also the enduring attachments that children and other individuals make to particular others. In this theory the key concept is that of behavioural system. This is conceived on the analogy of a physiological system organized homeostatically to ensure that a certain physiological measure, such as body temperature or blood pressure, is held between appropriate limits. In proposing the concept of a behavioural system to account for the way a child or older person maintains his relation to his attachment figure between certain limits of distance or accessibility, no more is done than to use these well-understood principles to account for a different form of homeostasis, namely one in which the set limits concern the organism's relation to clearly identified persons in, or other features of, the environment and in which the limits are maintained by behavioural instead of physiological means.

In thus postulating the existence of an internal psychological organization with a number of highly specific features, which include representational models of the self and of attachment figure(s), the theory proposed can be seen as having all the same basic properties as those that characterize other forms of structural theory, of which the variants of psychoanalysis are some of the best known, and that differentiate them so sharply from behaviourism in its many forms. Historically attachment theory was developed as a variant of object-relations theory.

The reason why in this account I have given so much space to the concept and theory of attachment is that, once those principles are grasped, there is little difficulty in understanding how the many other phenomena of central concern to clinicians are explained within the framework proposed.

Separation anxiety

For example, a new light is thrown on the problem of separation anxiety, namely anxiety about losing, or becoming separated from, someone loved. Why 'mere separation' should cause anxiety has been a mystery. Freud wrestled with the problem and advanced a number of hypotheses (Freud 1926; Strachey 1959).

29

Every other leading analyst has done the same. With no means of evaluating them, many divergent schools of thought have proliferated.

The problem lies, I believe, in an unexamined assumption, made not only by psychoanalysts but by more traditional psychiatrists as well, that fear is aroused in a mentally healthy person only in situations that everyone would perceive as intrinsically painful or dangerous, or that are perceived so by a person only because of his having become conditioned to them. Since fear of separation and loss does not fit this formula, analysts have concluded that what is feared is really some other situation; and a great variety of hypotheses have been advanced.

The difficulties disappear, however, when an ethological approach is adopted. For it then becomes evident that man, like other animals, responds with fear to certain situations, not because they carry a *high* risk of pain or danger, but because they signal an *increase* of risk. Thus, just as animals of many species, including man, are disposed to respond with fear to sudden movement or a marked change in level of sound or light because to do so has survival value, so are many species, including man, disposed to respond to separation from a potentially caregiving figure and for the same reasons.

When separation anxiety is seen in this light, as a basic human disposition, it is only a small step to understand why it is that threats to abandon a child, often used as a means of control, are so very terrifying. Such threats, and also threats of suicide by a parent, are, we now know, common causes of intensified separation anxiety. Their extraordinary neglect in traditional clinical theory is due, I suspect, not only to an inadequate theory of separation anxiety but to a failure to give proper weight to the powerful effects, at all ages, of real-life events.

Not only do threats of abandonment create intense anxiety but they also arouse anger, often also of intense degree, especially in older children and adolescents. This anger, the function of which is to dissuade the attachment figure from carrying out the threat, can easily become dysfunctional. It is in this light, I believe, that we can understand such absurdly paradoxical behaviour as the adolescent, reported by Burnham (1965), who, having murdered his mother, exclaimed, 'I couldn't stand to have her leave me.'

Other pathogenic family situations are readily understood in terms of attachment theory. One fairly common example is when a child has such a close relationship with his mother that he has difficulty in developing a social life outside the family, a relationship sometimes described as symbiotic. In a majority of such cases the cause of the trouble can be traced to the mother who, having grown up anxiously attached as a result of a difficult childhood, is now seeking to make her own child her attachment figure. So far from the child being over-indulged, as is sometimes asserted, he is being burdened with having to care for his own mother. Thus, in these cases, the normal relationship of attached child to caregiving parent is found to be inverted.

Mourning

Whilst separation anxiety is the usual response to a threat or some other risk of loss, mourning is the usual response to a loss after it has occurred. During the early years of psychoanalysis a number of analysts identified losses, occurring during childhood or in later life, as playing a causal role in emotional disturbance, especially in depressive disorders; and by 1950 a number of theories about the nature of mourning, and other responses to loss, had been advanced. Moreover, much sharp controversy had already been engendered. This controversy, which began during the thirties, arose from the divergent theories about infant development that had been elaborated in Vienna and London. Representative examples of the different points of view about mourning are those expressed in Helene Deutsch's *Absence of Grief* (1937) and Melanie Klein's *Mourning and its Relation to Manic-Depressive States* (1940). Whereas Deutsch held that, due to inadequate psychic development, children are unable to mourn, Klein held that they not only can mourn but do. In keeping with her strong emphasis on feeding, however, she held that the object mourned was the lost breast; and, in addition, she attributed a complex fantasy-life to the infant. Opposite though these theoretical positions are, both were constructed using the same methodology, namely by inferences about earlier phases of psychological development based on observations made during the analysis of older, and emotionally disturbed, subjects. Neither theory had been checked by direct observation of how ordinary children of different ages respond to a loss.

Approaching the problem prospectively, as I did, led me to different conclusions. During the early nineteen-fifties Robertson and I had generalized the sequence of responses seen in young children during temporary separation from mother as those of protest, despair, and detachment (Robertson and Bowlby 1952). A few years later, when reading a study by Marris (1958) of how widows respond to loss of husband, I was struck by the similarity of the responses he describes to those of young children. This led me to a systematic study of the literature on mourning, especially the mourning of healthy adults. The sequence of responses that commonly occur, it became clear, was very different from what clinical theorists had been assuming. Not only does mourning in mentally healthy adults last far longer than the six months often suggested in those days, but several component responses widely regarded as pathological were found to be common in healthy mourning. These include anger, directed at third parties, the self, and sometimes at the person lost, disbelief that the loss has occurred (misleadingly termed denial), and a tendency, often though not always unconscious, to search for the lost person in the hope of reunion. The clearer the picture of mourning responses in adults became, the clearer became their similarities to the responses observed in childhood. This conclusion, when first advanced (Bowlby 1960, 1961), was much criticized; but it has now been amply supported by a number of subsequent studies (e.g. Parkes 1972; Kliman 1965; Furman 1974; Raphael 1982).

Once an accurate picture of healthy mourning has been obtained, it becomes possible to identify features that are truly indicative of pathology. It becomes possible also to discern many of the conditions that promote healthy mourning and those that lead in a pathological direction. The belief that children are unable to mourn can then be seen to derive from generalizations that had been made from the analyses of children whose mourning had followed an atypical course. In many cases this had been due either to the child never having been given adequate information about what had happened, or else to there having been no one to sympathize with him and help him gradually come to terms with his loss, his yearning for his lost parent, his anger, and his sorrow.

Defensive processes

The next step in this reformulation of theory was to consider how defensive processes could best be conceptualized, a crucial step since defensive processes have always been at the heart of psychoanalytic theory. Although as a clinician I have inevitably been concerned with the whole range of defences, as a research worker I have directed my attention especially to the way a young child behaves towards his mother after a spell in a hospital or residential nursery unvisited. In such circumstances it is common for a child to begin by treating his mother almost as though she were a stranger, but then, after an interval, usually of hours or days, to become intensely clinging, anxious lest he lose her again, and angry with her should he think he may. In some way all his feeling for his mother and all the behaviour towards her we take for granted, keeping within range of her and most notably turning to her when frightened or hurt, have suddenly vanished – only to reappear again after an interval. That was the condition James Robertson and I termed detachment and which we believed was a result of some defensive process operating within the child.

Whereas Freud in his scientific theorizing felt confined to a conceptual model that explained all phenomena, whether physical or biological, in terms of the disposition of energy, today we have available conceptual models of much greater variety. Many draw on such interrelated concepts as organization, pattern, and information; while the purposeful activities of biological organisms can be conceived in terms of control systems structured in certain ways. With supplies of physical energy available to them, these systems become active on receipt of certain sorts of signal and inactive on receipt of signals of other sorts. Thus the world of science in which we live is radically different from the world Freud lived in at the turn of the century, and the concepts available to us immeasurably better suited to our problems than were the very restricted ones available in his day.

If we return now to the strange detached behaviour a young child shows after being away for a time with strange people in a strange place, what is so peculiar about it is, of course, the absence of attachment behaviour in circumstances in which we would confidently expect to see it. Even when he has hurt himself severely, such a child shows no sign of seeking comfort. Thus signals that would ordinarily activate attachment behaviour are failing to do so. This suggests that in some way and for some reason these signals are failing to reach the behavioural system responsible for attachment behaviour, that they are being blocked off, and the behavioural system itself is thereby immobilized. What this means is that a system controlling such crucial behaviour as attachment can in certain circumstances be rendered either temporarily or permanently incapable of being activated, and with it the whole range of feeling and desire that normally accompanies it is rendered incapable of being aroused.

In considering how this deactivation might be effected I turn to the work of the cognitive psychologists (e.g. Norman 1976; Dixon 1971, 1981) who, during the past twenty years, have revolutionized our knowledge of how we perceive the world and how we construe the situations we are in. Amongst much else that is clinically congenial, this revolution in cognitive theory not only gives unconscious mental processes the central place in mental life that analysts have always claimed for them, but presents a picture of the mental apparatus as being well able to shut off information of certain specified types and of doing so selectively without the person being aware of what is happening.

In the emotionally detached children described earlier and also, I believe, in adults who have developed the kind of personality that Winnicott (1960) describes as 'false self' and Kohut (1977) as 'narcissistic', the information being blocked off is of a very special type. So far from its being the routine exclusion of irrelevant and potentially distracting information that we engage in all the time and that is readily reversible, what are being excluded in these pathological conditions are the signals, arising from both inside and outside the person, that would activate their attachment behaviour and that would enable them both to love and to experience being loved. In other words, the mental structures responsible for routine selective exclusion are being employed – one might say exploited – for a special and potentially pathological purpose. This form of exclusion I refer to – for obvious reasons – as defensive exclusion, which is, of course, only another way of describing repression. And, just as Freud regarded repression as the key process in every form of defence, so I see the role of defensive exclusion.* A fuller account of this, an information-processing approach to the problem of defence, in which defences are classified into defensive processes, defensive beliefs, and defensive activities, is given in an early chapter of *Loss* (Bowlby 1980).

An alternative framework

During the time it has taken to develop the conceptual framework described here Margaret Mahler has been concerned with many of the same clinical problems and some of the same features of children's behaviour; and she also has been developing a revised conceptual framework to account for them, set out fully in her book *The Psychological Birth of the Human Infant* (Mahler, Pine, and Bergman 1975). To compare alternative frameworks is never easy, as Kuhn (1962) emphasizes, and no attempt is made to do so here. Elsewhere (e.g. Bowlby 1981) I describe what I believe to be some of the strengths of the framework I favour, including its close relatedness to empirical data, both clinical and developmental, and its compatibility with current ideas in evolutionary biology and neurophysiology; whilst what I see as the shortcomings of Mahler's framework are trenchantly criticized by Peterfreund (1978) and Klein (1981).

In brief, Mahler's theories of normal development, including her postulated normal phases of autism and symbiosis, are shown to rest not on observation but on preconceptions based on traditional psychoanalytic theory and, in doing so, to ignore

---

* As Spiegel (1981) points out, my term 'defensive exclusion' carries a meaning very similar to Sullivan's term 'selective inattention'.

almost entirely the remarkable body of new information about early infancy that has been built up from careful empirical studies over the past two decades. Although some of the clinical implications of Mahler's theory are not very different from those of attachment theory, and her concept of return to base to 'refuel' is similar to that of use of an attachment figure as a secure base from which to explore, the key concepts with which the two frameworks are built are very different.

Research

Nothing has been so rewarding as the immense amount of careful research to which the early work on maternal deprivation has given rise. The literature is now enormous and far beyond the compass of an account of this sort to summarize. Fortunately, moreover, it is unnecessary since a comprehensive and critical review of the field has been published by Rutter (1979) who concludes by referring to the 'continuing accumulation of evidence showing the importance of deprivation and disadvantage on children's psychological development' and expressing the view that the original arguments 'have been amply confirmed'. A principal finding of recent work is the extent to which two or more adverse experiences interact so that the risk of a psychological disturbance following is multiplied, often many times over. An example of this interactive effect of adverse experiences is seen in the findings of Brown and Harris (1978) derived from their studies of depressive disorders in women. (During the last decade this group has published many further findings of the greatest interest, see Harris (in press).)

Not only is there this strongly interactive effect of adverse experiences but there is an increased likelihood for someone who has had one adverse experience to have another. For example, 'people brought up in unhappy or disrupted homes are more likely to have illegitimate children, to become teenage mothers, to make unhappy marriages, and to divorce' (Rutter 1979). Thus adverse childhood experiences have effects of at least two kinds. First they make the individual more vulnerable to later adverse experiences. Secondly they make it more likely that he or she will meet with further such experiences. Whereas the earlier adverse experiences are likely to be wholly independent of the agency of the individual concerned, the later ones are likely to be the consequences of his or her own actions, actions that spring from those disturbances of personality to which the earlier experiences have given rise.

Of the many types of psychological disturbance that are traceable, at least in part, to one or another pattern of maternal deprivation, the effects on parental behaviour and thereby on the next generation are potentially the most serious. Thus a mother who, due to adverse experiences during childhood, grows up to be anxiously attached is prone to seek care from her own child and thereby lead the child to become anxious, guilty, and perhaps phobic (see review in Bowlby 1973). A mother who as a child suffered neglect and frequent severe threats of being abandoned or beaten is more prone than others to abuse her child physically (DeLozier 1982), resulting in the adverse effects on the child's developing personality recorded, amongst others, by George and Main (1979). Systematic research into the effects of childhood experiences on the way mothers and fathers treat their children has only just begun and seems likely to be one of the most fruitful of all fields for further research. Other research leads are described in a recent symposium edited by Parkes and Stevenson-Hinde (1982).

My reason for giving so much space in this account to the development of theory is not only because it has occupied so much of my time but because, as Kurt Lewin remarked long ago, 'There is nothing so practical as a good theory', and, of course, nothing so handicapping as a poor one. Without good theory as a guide, research is likely to be difficult to plan and to be unproductive, and findings are difficult to interpret. Without a reasonably valid theory of psychopathology, therapeutic techniques tend to be blunt and of uncertain benefit. Without a reasonably valid theory of aetiology, systematic and agreed measures of prevention will never be supported. My hope is that in the long term the greatest value of the theory proposed may prove to be the light it throws on the conditions most likely to promote healthy personality development. Only when those conditions are clear beyond doubt will parents know what is best for their children and will communities be willing to help them provide it.

LECTURE 3

Psychoanalysis as art and science

During the summer of 1978 I was invited to give a number of lectures in Canada. Among the invitations was one from the Canadian Psychoanalytic Society to give their academic lecture to the annual meeting of the Society to be held in Quebec City. The topic I selected is one which had concerned me for some years, and about which I believe there is still a great deal of confused thinking.

In taking as my theme psychoanalysis as art *and* science I want to draw attention to what I believe to be two very different aspects of our discipline – the art of psychoanalytic therapy and the science of psychoanalytic psychology – and in doing so to emphasize, on the one hand, the distinctive value of each and, on the other, the gulf that divides them – in regard both to the contrasting criteria by which each should be judged and the very different mental outlook that each demands. In emphasizing these distinctions, I cannot help regretting that the word *psychoanalysis* came early to be used ambiguously as Freud himself described it. 'While it was originally the name of a particular therapeutic method', he writes in his autobiography (1925), 'it has now also become the name of a science – the science of unconscious mental processes'.

The distinction I am drawing, of course, is not confined to psychoanalysis. It applies in every field in which the practice of a profession or a craft gives birth to a body of scientific knowledge – the blacksmith to metallurgy, the civil engineer to soil mechanics, the farmer to plant physiology, and the physician to the medical sciences. In each of these fields the roles differentiate. On the one hand are the practitioners, on the other the scientists, with a limited number of individuals attempting to combine both roles. As history shows, this process of differentiation often proves painful and misunderstandings are frequent. Since I believe differentiation is bound to come also in our own field, and is perhaps already overdue, let us consider some of the difficulties and misunderstandings to which it may all too easily give rise in the hope of avoiding them or mitigating their consequences.

I start by contrasting the roles of practitioner and research scientist and do so under three headings, using the case of medicine as an example.

Focus of study

The aim of the practitioner is to take into account as many aspects as he can of each and every clinical problem with which he is called upon to deal. This requires him not only to apply any scientific principle that appears relevant but also to draw on such personal experience of the condition as he may have acquired and, especially, to attend to that unique combination of features met with in each patient. Knowing how greatly patients differ, the experienced clinician recognizes that a form of treatment well suited to one would be totally inappropriate to another. Taking all factors into account and giving each its due weight is the art of clinical judgement.

The outlook of the research scientist is quite different. In his efforts to discern general patterns underlying individual variety he ignores the particular and strives to simplify, risking thereby over-simplification. If he is wise he will probably concentrate attention on a limited aspect of a limited problem. If in making his selection he proves sagacious, or simply lucky, he may not only elucidate the problem selected but also develop ideas applicable to a broader range. If his selection proves unwise or unlucky he may merely end up knowing more and more about less and less. That is the risk every researcher runs. The art of research lies in selecting a limited manageable problem and the methods that will best help solve it. This brings me to my second point.

Modes of acquiring information

In the methods available to him for acquiring information the practitioner has certain great advantages over the research scientist but also certain great disadvantages. Let us start with the advantages.

In his role of giving help the practitioner is permitted access to information of certain kinds that remain closed to the scientist: as a friend of mine is fond of saying, it's only surgeons who are allowed to cut you open to see what's inside. In an analogous way it is only by treating a patient therapeutically that a psychoanalyst is given access to much of importance going on in a person's mind. In both professions, moreover, practitioners are permitted to intervene in specified ways and privileged to observe what the consequences of such interventions are. These are immense advantages and psychoanalysts have not been slow to exploit them.

Yet no science can prosper for long without enlisting new methods to cross-check on observations made and on hypotheses born of older methods. Here the research scientist is likely to have the advantage. In the medical sciences, physiologists and pathologists have made immense advances by means of animal experiments, tissue culture, biochemical analyses, and a thousand other ingenious techniques. Indeed, it is a hallmark of a creative scientist that he devises new means by which phenomena, perhaps already well studied by other methods, can be observed in some new way.

It is in this area, I believe, that the ambiguous use of the word psychoanalysis has done greatest harm. For it has led some analysts to suppose that the only method of enquiry appropriate for the advancement of psychoanalytic science is that of treating a patient psychoanalytically. Since I believe this to be a profound misunderstanding I shall be saying a good deal more about it. Before doing so, however, I want to say a word about the place of scepticism and faith in the respective worlds of scientist and practitioner.

Scepticism and faith

In his day-to-day work it is necessary for a scientist to exercise a high degree of criticism and self-criticism: and in the world he inhabits neither the data nor the theories of a leader, however admired personally he may be, are exempt from challenge and criticism. There is no place for authority.

The same is not true in the practice of a profession. If he is to be effective a practitioner must be prepared to act as though certain principles and certain theories were valid; and in deciding which to adopt he is likely to be guided by those with experience from whom he learns. Since, moreover, there is a tendency in all of us to be impressed whenever the application of a theory appears to have been successful, practitioners are at special risk of placing greater confidence in a theory than the evidence available may justify.

From the standpoint of clinical practice this is no bad thing. On the contrary, there is abundant evidence that the great majority of patients are helped by the faith and hope that a practitioner brings to his work; whilst it is often the very lack of these qualities that makes so many excellent research workers sadly ill-suited to be therapists.

Yet, though faith in the validity of *particular* data and in *particular* theories is out of place in a scientist, I do not wish to imply that he is nothing but a sceptic. On the contrary, his whole way of living is founded on faith, faith that in the long run the best route to reliable knowledge is the application of scientific method.

I am, of course, aware that there are many psychoanalysts who do not share this faith and who believe that the types of problem with which we deal lie far outside the scope of science. This is a view I respect, though I do not share: nor, of course, did Freud. Yet even those of us who are most enthusiastic about applying scientific method in our field must recognize that there may well be problems that it can never solve. We simply do not know. Our task, as I see it, is to apply our method as skilfully as we can, on the one hand believing that the area of reliable knowledge will thereby be expanded and, on the other, accepting that there are likely always to remain still greater areas lying beyond the scope of any existing mode of scientific enquiry.

To many of you, I am afraid, engaged in therapeutic practice but also hoping to contribute to the advance of psychoanalytic science, the contrasts I am drawing between the roles of practitioner and scientist will hardly be welcome. Yet I believe that it is only by recognizing these differences and acting accordingly that the strengths of each role can be used to fullest advantage – or that any one person can occupy both of them with any hope of success. As practitioners we deal in complexity; as scientists we strive to simplify. As practitioners we use theory as a guide; as scientists we challenge that same theory. As practitioners we accept restricted modes of enquiry; as scientists we enlist every method we can.

Earlier I remarked on the need for every developing science to devise new methods for obtaining data. The reason for this is that, however productive any one method may be, it is bound to have its limitations, whilst there is always a prospect that some other method may compensate for them. Thus the new method may be in no way superior to the old; indeed it may have great limitations. Its usefulness lies simply in the fact that its strengths and its limitations are different. Perhaps I can illustrate the point by reference to my own work.

When I qualified in psychoanalysis in 1937, members of the British Society were occupied in exploring the fantasy worlds of adults and children, and it was regarded as almost outside the proper interest of an analyst to give systematic attention to a person's real experiences. That was a time when Freud's famous about-turn of 1897 regarding the aetiology of hysteria* had led to the view that anyone who places emphasis on what a child's *real experiences* may have been, and perhaps still are being, was regarded as pitifully naïve. Almost by definition

---

* Efron (1977) has discussed the circumstances in which Freud's abrupt change of mind took place.

it was assumed that anyone interested in the external world could not be interested in the internal world, indeed was almost certainly running away from it.

To me as a biologist this contrast of internal with external, of organism with environment, never appealed. Furthermore, as a psychiatrist engaged in work with children and families and deeply influenced by the insights of two analytically oriented social workers, I was daily confronted with the impact on children of the emotional problems from which their parents suffered. Here are two examples I still recall vividly. In one a father was deeply concerned about his 8-year-old son's masturbation and in reply to my enquiries explained how, whenever he caught him with his hand on his genitals, he put him under a cold tap. This led me to ask father whether he himself had ever had any worry about masturbation, and he launched into a long and pathetic tale of how he had battled with the problem all his life. In another case a mother's punitive treatment of her 3-year-old's jealousy of the new baby was as quickly traced to the problem she had always had with her own jealousy of a younger brother.

Observations of these kinds led me to conclude that it is just as necessary for analysts to study the way a child is really treated by his parents as it is to study the internal representations he has of them, indeed that the principal focus of our studies should be the interaction of the one with the other, of the internal with the external. Believing that that would be possible only if we had far more systematic knowledge about the effects on a child of the experiences he has during his early years within his family, I concentrated my attention on this area. The reasons that I selected as my special field of study the removal of a young child from his home to a residential nursery or hospital rather than the broader field of parent–child interaction were several. First it was an event that I believed could have serious ill effects on a child's personality development. Secondly there could be no debate whether it had occurred or not, in this regard contrasting strongly with the difficulty of obtaining valid information about how a parent treats a child. Thirdly it appeared to be a field in which preventive measures might be possible. And perhaps I should add, fourthly, that I was stimulated by the sheer incredulity with which my views were met by some, though by no means all, of my colleagues when I first advanced them just before the war.

The results of our ensuing studies, undertaken by two researchers both of whom subsequently qualified as analysts, James Robertson and Christoph Heinicke, are now well-known; and I believe them to have had a significant effect on psychoanalytic thinking. The points I wish to make now, however, concern research strategy. Despite the pioneer work of such distinguished analysts as Anna Freud, René Spitz, Ernst Kris, Margaret Mahler, and others, for long there has been a tendency in analytic circles to regard the direct observation of young children and the recording of what they say as no more than an auxiliary method of research, the results of which are of interest when they confirm conclusions already reached by the traditional method of treating patients but which are unable to contribute anything original. The notion that the direct observation of children – in and out of the family setting – is not only a valuable method for advancing psychoanalytic science but is indispensable to it has been slow to be accepted.

The principal contributions of these direct studies, I believe, are to cast light on how children develop emotionally and socially, on what the ranges of variation are in respect to a very large number of relevant parameters, and what types of family experience tend to influence children to develop in one way rather than another. Let me give some examples of findings by colleagues working in our sister sciences of ethology and developmental psychology that I believe to be highly germane to our clinical understanding.

The first example is from the work of Mary Salter Ainsworth (1977), formerly at Johns Hopkins University and now at the University of Virginia. Trained initially as a clinical psychologist, Mary Ainsworth worked with us at the Tavistock during the early fifties and then spent a couple of years studying mothers and infants in Uganda. Her definitive study has concerned the development of mother–infant interaction during the first year of life in white middle-class homes in Baltimore, Maryland. She has had a personal analysis and is keenly alive to the types of problem analysts regard as important.

During her study of mothers and infants in Uganda Ainsworth was struck how infants, once mobile, commonly use mother as a base from which to explore. When conditions are favourable an infant moves away from mother on exploratory excursions and returns to her again from time to time. By eight months of age almost every infant observed who had had a stable mother-figure to whom to become attached showed this behaviour; but, should mother be absent, such organized excursions became much less evident or ceased. As a result of these and similar findings, both for human and for monkey infants, the notion has been developed that an ordinary devoted mother provides a child with a secure base from which he can explore and to which he can return when upset or frightened. Similar observations, of course, have been made by Margaret Mahler (Mahler, Pine, and Bergman 1975), though she interprets them in terms of a theoretical framework different to the one which Ainsworth and I use. This concept of the secure personal base, from which a child, an adolescent, or an adult goes out to explore and to which he returns from time to time, is one I have come to regard as crucial for an understanding of how an emotionally stable person develops and functions *all through his life.*

In her project in Baltimore, Ainsworth was not only able to study this kind of behaviour more closely but described many individual variations of it to be seen in a sample of twenty-three infants at 12 months of age. Observations were made of the infants' exploratory and attachment behaviour, and the balance between them, both when the infants were at home with mother and also when they were placed in a slightly strange test situation. In addition, having obtained data on the type of mothering each infant had been receiving throughout his first year of life (by means of prolonged observation sessions at three weekly intervals in the child's home), Ainsworth was in a position to propose hypotheses linking certain types of emotional and behavioural development at 12 months with certain types of preceding mothering experience.

The findings of the study (see the review by Ainsworth, 1977) show that the way a particular infant of 12 months behaves with and without his mother at home and the way he behaves with and without her in a slightly strange test situation have much in common. Drawing on observations of behaviour in both types of situation it is then possible to classify the infants into three main groups, according to two criteria: (a) how much or how little they explore when with mother or without her, and (b) how they treat mother – when she is present, when she departs, and, especially, when she returns.

There were eight children whose overall behaviour at their first birthday Ainsworth was disposed to regard as promising well for the future. Such infants explored actively, especially in mother's presence, and used mother as a base by keeping note of her whereabouts, exchanging glances, and from time to time returning to her to share in enjoyable mutual contact. When mother had been absent for a short time she was greeted warmly on her return. I will call these group X.

There were no less than eleven children whose overall behaviour gave cause for concern and whom I will call group Z. Three of them were passive, both at home and in the test situation; they explored little and, instead, sucked a thumb or rocked. Constantly anxious about mother's whereabouts, they cried much in her absence but were contrary and difficult on her return. The other eight in this group alternated between appearing very independent and ignoring mother altogether, and then suddenly becoming anxious and trying to find her. Yet, when they did find her, they seemed not to enjoy contact with her, and often they struggled to get away again. In fact, they presented a classical picture of ambivalence.

The remaining four of the twenty-three children studied were judged to occupy a position intermediate between those given a good prognosis on their first birthday and those given a guarded one. I will call them group Y.

Since every three weeks throughout these infants' short lives the researchers had spent a three-hour session in the child's home observing and recording mother and infant behaviour, they had much first-hand data from which to rate a mother's behaviour towards her child. In making these ratings Ainsworth used four distinct nine-point rating scales; but, since ratings on these scales intercorrelate highly, for present purposes one scale is sufficient – a scale that measures the degree of sensitivity or insensitivity that a mother shows to her baby's signals and communications. Whereas a sensitive mother seems constantly to be 'tuned in' to receive her baby's signals, is likely to interpret them correctly, and to respond to them both promptly and appropriately, an insensitive mother will often not notice her baby's signals, will misinterpret them when she does notice them, and will then respond tardily, inappropriately, or not at all. When the ratings on this scale for the mothers of infants in each of the three groups are examined, it is found that the mothers of the eight infants in group X are rated uniformly high (range 5.5 to 9.0), those of the eleven infants in group Z are rated uniformly low (range 1.0 to 3.5), and those of the four in group Y are in the middle (range 4.5 to 5.5). Differences are statistically significant.

Plainly a great deal of further work is necessary before it is possible to draw conclusions with any high degree of confidence. Nevertheless, the overall patterns of personality development and of mother–child interaction visible at 12 months are sufficiently similar to what is seen of personality development and of parent–child interaction in later years for it to be plausible to believe that the one is the forerunner of the other. At the least, Ainsworth's findings show that an infant, whose mother is sensitive, accessible, and responsive to him, who accepts his behaviour and is co-operative in dealing with him, is far from being the demanding and unhappy child that some theories might suggest. Instead, mothering of this sort is evidently compatible with a child who is developing a limited measure of self-reliance by the time of his first birthday combined with a high degree of trust in his mother and enjoyment of her company.

Conversely mothers who are insensitive to their children's signals, perhaps because they are preoccupied and worried about other things, who ignore their children, or interfere with their activities in an arbitrary way, or simply reject them, are likely to have children who are unhappy or anxious or difficult. Anyone who has worked in a clinic seeing disturbed children or adolescents will hardly be surprised by that.

Although Ainsworth's finding of a correlation between a mother's responsiveness to her infant and the infant's way of behaving towards her at 12 months is highly significant statistically and has been confirmed by subsequent studies, it is always possible to argue that the partner who plays the greater role in determining whether interaction develops happily or not is the infant and not the mother. Some infants are born difficult, so the argument runs, and the mothers' adverse reactions to them are only to be expected.

I do not think the evidence supports this view. For example, the observations made during the first three months of these infants' lives showed no correlation between the amount of crying a baby did and the way his mother was treating him; whereas by the end of the first year mothers who had attended promptly to their crying babies had babies who cried much less than did the babies of mothers who had left them to cry.

There are other findings, some of which are referred to in Lecture 6, that also support the view that in all but a small minority of cases it is the mother who is mainly responsible for how interaction develops.

Drawing on her own home observations, Ainsworth has given a graphic account of what can happen. For example, she describes how she has sat in homes hearing a baby crying and crying and counted the minutes until the mother has responded. In some cases a mother sits it out as long as she can bear to, believing that it would be bad for the baby and make him cry more were she to attend to him – a belief that Ainsworth's findings firmly disprove. In other cases a mother may be too engaged in something else to go. In yet others it appears as though a mother has altogether failed to register that her baby is crying – a situation an observer finds extremely painful to sit through. Usually these are women suffering from anxiety and depression and who are really incapable of attending to anything else.

Now it will be evident to everyone that detailed and accurate observations of these kinds, which demonstrate how enormously different the experiences of different children can be, are obtainable only by the methods used by these researchers. Had the observers not been present to see and hear what was going on but had relied instead on what the mothers told them, the pictures they would have got would in many cases have been entirely false; and all hope of finding significant correlations between the way a child develops and the way he is treated by his mother and father would have vanished. Yet, as we have seen, when reliable methods of observation are used, even with quite small samples, highly significant correlations are found.

In emphasizing the determining role a mother plays in setting the pattern of interaction with her baby, to which I believe the evidence clearly points, I lay no blame. Looking after a baby, or a toddler, or an older child for that matter, is not only a skilled job but also a very hard and exacting one. Even for a woman who has had a happy childhood and who is now enjoying the help and support of her husband, and perhaps also of her own mother, and who has not been filled with mistaken advice about the dangers of spoiling her baby, it is a taxing one. That a woman with none of these advantages gets into an emotional hassle is hardly surprising and certainly not an occasion for blame. Yet there now seems little doubt that when infants and young children are the subjects of insensitive mothering, mixed perhaps with occasions of outright rejection, and later to separations and threats of separation the effects are deplorable. Such experiences greatly increase a child's fear of losing his mother, increase his demands for her presence and also his anger at her absences, and may also lead him to despair of ever having a secure and loving relationship with anyone.

Although ideas of this sort are much more familiar and also more acceptable in analytic circles today than they were a generation ago, thanks to the influence of Balint, Fairbairn, Winnicott, and many others, I am inclined to think that their implications, both for theory and for practice, are still a long way from being digested.

Let me illustrate the point by considering the aetiological and therapeutic problems presented by the type of patient who in the United Kingdom is likely to be described as a schizoid personality (Fairbairn 1940) or as having a false self (Winnicott 1960) and in North America as being a borderline personality or suffering from pathological narcissism (e.g. Kohut 1971; Kernberg 1975).

The picture such a person presents is one of assertive independence and emotional self-sufficiency. On no account is he going to be beholden to anyone and, in so far as he enters into relationships at all, he makes sure he retains control. For much of the time he may appear to manage wonderfully well, but there may be times when he becomes depressed or develops psychosomatic symptoms, often for no reason he knows of. Only should symptoms or a bout of depression become severe is there any possibility of his seeking treatment, and then more likely than not he will prefer drugs to analysts.

When such a person does come for analysis he is careful to keep the analyst at arm's length and to control what happens. What he tells us is lucid, but he avoids any reference to feeling, except perhaps to say how bored he gets. Holidays or other interruptions he welcomes as saving his time. Perhaps he finds the analysis an 'interesting exercise'; although he is not convinced it is much use. And in any case he could probably do a better job by analysing himself!

There is, of course, a large literature discussing the psychopathology of these conditions and the therapeutic problems they present; but on whatever issues there may be agreement there is none on aetiology. To take two contrasting viewpoints: whereas Winnicott (1960, 1974) attributes the condition squarely to early environmental failure in the form of 'not good enough mothering', Kernberg (1975) in his systematic treatise gives no more than a couple of easily missed paragraphs to the possible role that mothering plays in influencing development, and only a few passing references to the inadequate mothering certain of his patients may have received. That early experience may play the key role in determining these conditions is not seriously examined by him.

Plainly it is of the greatest importance that in due course we should reach some consensus about this matter; and in debating the issues I believe we should be foolish not to take account of data from as many sources as we can tap. For some conditions epidemiological surveys are now proving informative but I doubt whether they have anything yet to tell us about this one. At present therefore we have to make do with data from our two familiar sources: (a) the analytic treatment of patients, (b) the direct observation of young children with their mothers.

As regards data obtained during treatment, I suspect it would be fruitful for some open-minded person to survey the psychoanalytic literature and draw together all the case reports which record information about the childhood experiences of these patients. My guess is that, in so far as any information is given, it would strongly support Winnicott's view that these patients have had disturbed childhoods in which inadequate mothering in one form or another – and it can take many – bulks large. Since I have made no such survey, I can do no more than illustrate the kind of findings that I would confidently expect. The following details come from case reports published by three analysts each much influenced by Winnicott's views.

One report is by Donald Winnicott's widow Clare Winnicott (1980). The patient, a professional woman of 41, presented a classical picture of the emotionally self-sufficient personality who recently had developed a variety of psychosomatic symptoms. Only after a good deal of analysis did she divulge the events of her childhood. Since her mother was in full-time work, she was looked after by a German girl who left suddenly when the patient was 2½. Then, after six months of uncertainty, she was taken by her mother to have tea with a friend and later found her mother had disappeared and she was alone in a strange bed. Next day she was taken to the boarding school where her mother's friend worked as matron, and she stayed there till she was 9, usually spending the holidays there also. She appears to have settled in well (ominous words!) and coped very success-fully; but from that time forward her emotional life had dried up.

A second report, by Jonathan Pedder (1976), is of a young teacher in her mid-twenties whose personality and symptoma-tology bear a strong resemblance to Clare Winnicott's patient. Although at the initial interview she had given an idealized picture of her childhood, it soon emerged that at the age of 18 months she had been sent to stay with an aunt during her mother's next pregnancy. After six months there she had come to feel that her aunt was more of a mother to her than was her real mother and she had found returning home a painful experience. Thereafter, until she was 10, she had been terrified of another separation; but then she had 'switched off' her anxiety 'like a tap', as she put it, and with the anxiety had disappeared most of her emotional life as well.

The third report, by Elizabeth Lind (1973), concerns a young graduate of 23 who, though severely depressed and planning suicide, maintained that his state of mind was less an illness than 'a philosophy of life'. He was the eldest of a large family; and by the time he was 3 two siblings had already been born. His parents, he said, quarrelled both frequently and violently. When the family was young, father had been working long hours away from home training for a profession. Mother was always unpredictable. Often she was so distraught by her quarrelling children that she would lock herself in her room for days on end. Several times she had left home, taking the daughters with her but leaving the sons behind.

He had been told that he had been an unhappy baby, a poor feeder and sleeper, who had often been left alone to cry for long periods. His crying, it was said, had been just an attempt to gain control of his parents and to be spoilt. On one occasion he had had appendicitis and he remembered lying awake all night moaning; but his parents had done nothing and by next morning he was seriously ill. Later, during therapy, he recalled how disturbed he used to be at hearing his younger brothers and sisters being left to cry and how he hated his parents for it and felt like killing them.

He had always felt like a lost child and had been puzzled to understand why he had been rejected. His first day at school, he said, had been the worst in his life. It had seemed a final rejection by his mother; all day he had felt desperate and had never stopped crying. After that he had gradually come to hide all desires for love and support: he had refused ever to ask for help or to have anything done for him.

Now, during therapy, he was frightened he might break down and cry and want to be mothered. This would lead his therapist, he felt sure, to regard him as a nuisance and his behaviour simply as attention-seeking; and, were he to say anything personal to her, he fully expected her to be offended and perhaps lock herself in her room.

In all three cases the patient's recent breakdown had followed the collapse of a significant but fragile relationship about which each member of the pair had had reservations and to the ending of which each of the patients had, him or herself, obviously contributed.

In treating these patients all three analysts adopted Winnicott's technique of permitting the free expression of what are traditionally termed 'dependency feelings', with the result that each patient in due course developed an intense and anxious attachment to his or her analyst (to use the terminology I prefer, (Bowlby 1969, 1973)). This enabled each patient to recover the emotional life he or she had lost during childhood and with it to recover a sense of 'real self'. Therapeutically the results were good.

Admittedly, the findings from these three cases prove nothing. Nevertheless they are suggestive and, so far as they go, support Winnicott's theory of aetiology. Even so it is always open to critics to cast doubt on the validity of what a patient recalls about his childhood and to question whether the sequence of events recounted had the effect on his feeling life that he so explicitly claims. (It is worth noting that the events that each of these three patients held to be a turning point had occurred after their second birthdays.)

Now it seems clear that the controversies about aetiology are never going to be settled as long as we rely solely on the retrospective and perhaps biased evidence derived from the analyses of patients, whether they be adults or children. What is needed is evidence of a *different* kind to provide some sort of cross-check. This is where I believe the direct observations of young children and their mothers are potentially so useful. Is there any evidence from that source that suggests that a child's feeling life can become numbed by the types of experience described? The answer, of course, is that there is a great deal.

Here naturally I point first to the observations made by James Robertson (1953) and confirmed later by Christoph Heinicke and Ilse Westheimer (1965) on how children between the ages of 12 and 36 months behave when removed from home to the care of strange people in a strange place, such as a residential nursery or hospital, with no one person to act as a mother-substitute. In such conditions a child comes in time to act as if neither mothering nor contact with humans has much significance for him. As his caretakers come and go he ceases to attach himself to anyone and after his return home stays remote from his parents for days, and perhaps for much longer if he is treated unsympathetically.

There is reason to believe, moreover, that a young child can develop this kind of defensive numbing in response to a mother who rejects him and without any major separation. Examples of this sequence are to be found in observations recorded by Mahler (1971). More definitive findings are reported by Mary Main (1977), a colleague of Mary Ainsworth's, who has made a special study of a group of children in the age-range 12 to 20 months, each of whom not only failed to greet his mother after she had left him with a stranger for a few minutes but deliberately avoided her. Viewing some of Main's videotaped records I was astonished to see to what lengths some of these children went. One approached her mother briefly but with head averted and then retreated from her. Another, instead of approaching his mother, placed himself facing into the corner of the room, as though complying with a punishment, and then knelt down with his face to the floor. In every case videotaped records of these mothers playing with their toddlers during a later session showed them to differ from the mothers of non-avoidant toddlers: they appeared 'angry, inexpressive and dis-liking of physical contact with the infant'. Some scolded in angry tones, some mocked, others spoke sarcastically to or about their child. An obvious possibility is that by keeping away from his mother in this way a child is avoiding being treated in a hostile way again.

Thus, so far as the cross-checks provided by direct obser-vations of young children and their mothers go, they tend to support a Winnicott-type theory. Put briefly, and in my own words, the child, and later the adult, becomes afraid to allow himself to become attached to anyone for fear of a further re-jection with all the agony, the anxiety, and the anger to which that would lead. As a result there is a massive block against his expressing or even feeling his natural desire for a close trusting relationship, for care, comfort, and love – which I regard as the subjective manifestations of a major system of instinctive behaviour.

An explanation of this kind, although much less complex than some proposed in the literature, accounts well for how these people behave both in the world at large and with ourselves as analysts. Inevitably they bring their fear of entering into a

55

trusting relationship with them to analysis, which we experience as a massive resistance. Then, when at length their feelings are recovered, they more than half expect that we shall treat them as they recall being treated by their parents. In consequence they live in dread of being rejected and become intensely angry should they suspect us of deserting them. Not infrequently, moreover, the way they treat us – with abuse and rejection – is found to be a version of the treatment to which they recall having themselves been subjected as children.

You will see that in the explanation of how these patients behave during analysis I have advanced a number of interlocking hypotheses. In a research programme each requires scrutiny and testing in the light of further data. Among the many methods that I would expect to prove of value is the study, in a therapeutic setting, of parents and children interacting with one another. In addition, there remains an important place for further observations to be made during the analysis of individual patients; though I believe that, if clinical research is to yield its full potential, it has to be pursued in a far more systematic and directed way than hitherto.

To give an example: it would be of value were a detailed record to be kept of the responses of one or more of these patients before and after each successive weekend, each vacation, and each unexpected interruption of the sessions, with an equally detailed record of how the analyst dealt with them. This would enable us to know the repertoire of responses a given patient presents on these occasions, and also the changes in response he presents over time. It would also be especially valuable if we were to have a detailed account of the conditions in which a major therapeutic change occurs. If, perhaps in a collaborative programme, records could be kept on a number of such patients, it might be possible to discover whether a frank and detailed discussion of the painful experiences a patient recalls having had in his relationships with his parents and the effects these appear to have had and still to be having on the ways he treats other people, including of course ourselves, promotes therapeutic change, as I predict, or hinders it, as is believed by some analysts.

Naturally, in embarking on this or any other research pro-

gramme an analyst must bear in mind his professional respon-
sibilities; for with patients who present a false self these can
be very onerous. Winnicott describes the 'period of extreme
dependence' through which such patients go during therapy
and gives warning that 'analysts who are not prepared to go and
meet the heavy needs of patients who become dependent in this
way must be careful so to choose their cases that they do not
include false self types'.

This brings me back to the art of therapy. To provide, by being
ourselves, the conditions in which a patient of this kind can
discover and recover what Winnicott calls his real self, and I
call his attachment desires and feelings, is not easy. On the
one hand, we have really to be trustworthy and we have also
genuinely to respect all those yearnings for affection and
intimacy that each of us has but which in these patients have
become lost. On the other, we must not offer more than we can
give and we must not move faster than the patient can bear. To
achieve this balance requires all the intuition, imagination, and
empathy of which we are capable. But it also requires a firm
grasp of what the patient's problems are and what we are trying
to do. This is why it is so very important that the problems of
aetiology and psychopathology should be clarified as far as the
application of scientific method makes possible and, further,
that analysts should be thoroughly informed about the whole
range of family experiences, from birth on through adolescence,
that, increasing evidence shows, affect how a child's emotional
life develops. Only when we become armed with that and much
further knowledge shall we be in a position to meet the exacting
demand that Freud makes in one of the last papers he wrote, in
which he draws attention to 'the kernel of truth' in a patient's
symptoms and to the therapeutic value of constructions in
analysis (1937). In it he writes: 'What we are in search of is a
picture of the patient's forgotten years that shall be alike trustworthy and in all essential respects complete.'

LECTURE 4

Psychoanalysis
as a natural science

*In the autumn of 1980 I was appointed Freud Memorial Visiting
Professor of Psychoanalysis at University College, London. In my
inaugural lecture I returned to the theme I had spoken on in Canada two
years previously. Having always believed that the body of knowledge
labelled psychoanalysis should become a part of natural science, I
was distressed by the pressure of the opposition. To accept that psychoanalysis should abandon its aim of becoming a natural science and
instead should regard itself as a hermeneutic discipline has seemed to me
to be not only a result of obsolete ideas about science but also a counsel of
despair; because, in a hermeneutic discipline, there are no criteria by the
application of which it is ever possible to resolve disagreement.*

*A problem encountered by every analyst who has proposed new
theoretical ideas is the criticism that the new theory is 'not psychoanalysis'. Such criticism turns, of course, on how we define psychoanalysis. Most unfortunately, defining it in terms of Freud's theories is
all too common. This is in contrast to the definitions adopted by
academic disciplines which are always in terms of the phenomena to be
studied and the problems to be solved. In such disciplines progress is
frequently signalled by changes of theory, sometimes of a revolutionary
kind. So long as analysts continue to define psychoanalysis in terms of
any particular theory, they must not complain that their discipline is
cold-shouldered by academics. Furthermore by so defining it they are
condemning it to frozen inertia.*

The following version of this lecture differs in a number of ways from

58

the original, in particular by abbreviating the discussion of issues already dealt with in the preceding lectures.

From 1895, when Freud made his first attempt to sketch a theoretical framework for psychoanalysis, until 1938, the year before he died, Freud was determined that his new discipline should conform to the requirements of a natural science. Thus, in the opening sentence of his *Project* he writes: 'The intention is to furnish a psychology that shall be a natural science. ...' (Freud 1950, 295); whilst in the *Outline* we find a passage in which he asserts that, once the concept of psychical processes being unconscious is granted, 'psychology is enabled to take its place as a natural science like any other' (Freud 1940, 158).

Admittedly during the intervening years Freud's ideas about the scope of his science had changed considerably from his early ambition 'to represent psychical processes as quantitatively determinate states of specifiable material particles' (1950, written in 1895) to his later definition of psychoanalysis as 'the science of unconscious mental processes' (1925). But from first to last there can be no doubt what sort of discipline Freud intended psychoanalysis to be.

Nevertheless, despite Freud's unwavering intention, the scientific status of psychoanalysis remains equivocal. On the one hand philosophers of science have dubbed it a pseudo-science on the grounds that, however large a measure of truth they may contain, psychoanalytic theories are cast in so elastic a form that they are unfalsifiable. On the other many psycho-analysts, disillusioned by the inadequacies of Freud's meta-psychology and preoccupied with the personal perspective which is unquestionably required in clinical work, have abandoned Freud's aims and claims and have declared that psychoanalysis is miscast as a science and should be conceived instead as one of the humanities, e.g. Home (1966), Ricoeur (1970), and others in Europe. Both Schafer (1976) and George Klein (1976), espousing this view, have advanced proposals alternative to Freud's: but each of their reformulations, different though they be, seems a version of *Hamlet* without the Prince. Gone are all concepts of causality and theories of biologically rooted impulse and, in Schafer's version, gone also are concepts of repression and unconscious mental activity.

Melanie Klein has made very different proposals, ones which certainly do not suffer from these defects; but it would be difficult to claim that the form they take or the research they have engendered meet scientific requirements.

Yet by no means do all analysts despair of developing their discipline as a natural science. Alive to the deficiencies of Freud's metapsychology, especially his concepts of psychic energy and drive, a few are attempting to replace it with a new conceptual framework consistent with current scientific thinking. Central to these new proposals are ideas drawn from systems theory and the study of human information processing. Those active in this enterprise include Rubinstein (1967), Peterfreund (1971, 1982), Rosenblatt and Thickstun (1977), Gedo (1979), and myself (1969, 1980). Meanwhile there are also a number of analysts who have been seeking to extend the discipline's data-base by studying children's social and emotional development using direct observations. Some of these studies have been atheoretical, e.g. Offer (1969). The authors of others have attempted to put new empirical wine into the old theoretical bottles, e.g. Spitz (1957), Mahler (Mahler, Pine, and Bergman 1975); whilst others again, e.g. Sander (1964, 1980), Stern (1977), and myself (1958, 1969, 1973), have searched for new theoretical models. My own search has led not only to control theory and information processing but also to the biologically rooted disciplines of ethology and comparative psychology. Thus there is no lack of new initiatives and it will take time to see which of them, or perhaps which combination of them, proves most productive of scientific advance. Here my aim is to describe one such initiative, my own, and why I think it promising.

In the preceding lecture I described the circumstances which led me to choose as a field of research the responses of a young child to being removed from his or her mother and placed for a time in a strange place with strange people, and how these observations led on to the formulation of attachment theory. Among essential features of this are that the human infant comes into the world genetically biased to develop a set of behavioural patterns that, given an appropriate environment, will result in his keeping more or less close proximity to whomever cares for him, and that this tendency to maintain proximity serves the function of protecting the mobile infant and growing child from a number of dangers, amongst which in man's environment of evolutionary adaptedness the danger of predation is likely to have been paramount.

A concept that emerged early from ethologically oriented studies of mother–child relationships (Ainsworth 1967) and which has proved of great clinical value is that of a mother, or mother-substitute, providing a child with a secure base from which he can explore. By the last months of the first year of life an infant brought up in an ordinary affectionate home is very clear whom he prefers to care for him, a preference especially evident should he be tired, frightened, or sick. Whoever that may be, and it is usually his mother, is then able by her very presence, or ready accessibility, to create the conditions which enable him to explore his world in a confident way. At the time of his second birthday, for example, a healthy child whose mother is resting on a garden seat will make a series of excursions away from her, each time returning to her before making the next excursion. On some occasions, when he returns, he simply smiles and makes his number; on others he leans against her knee; on yet others he wants to climb on her lap. But never does he stay for long unless he is frightened or tired or thinks she is about to leave. Anderson (1972), who made a study of this sort in a London park, observed that during the second and third years it is very rare for a child to go further than two hundred feet before returning. Should he lose sight of his mother, exploration is forgotten. His top priority then is to regain her, in an older child by searching and in a younger one by howling.

It is evident that there is no way of explaining this type of behaviour in terms of a build-up of psychic energy which is then discharged. An alternative model (already described in earlier lectures) is to think of the proximity keeping of a child as being mediated by a set of behavioural systems organized cybernetically. Activation is intensified in conditions of pain, fatigue, and anything frightening; and reduced by proximity to or contact with the mother-figure. We can then postulate that the behaviour that takes him away from his mother into the wide world, which is conveniently termed exploratory behaviour, is incompatible with attachment behaviour and has a lower priority. It is thus only when attachment behaviour is relatively inactive that exploration occurs.

As an individual grows older his life continues to be organized in the same kind of way, though his excursions become steadily longer both in time and space. On entering school they will last for hours and later for days. During adolescence they may last for weeks or months, and new attachment figures are likely to be sought. Throughout adult life the availability of a responsive attachment figure remains the source of a person's feeling secure. All of us, from the cradle to the grave, are happiest when life is organized as a series of excursions, long or short, from the secure base provided by our attachment figure(s).

In terms of the theoretical model proposed, the pronounced changes in the organization of attachment behaviour that occur during individual development are regarded as being due, in part, to the threshold for its activation being raised (perhaps through changes in endocrine levels) and, in part, to the control systems becoming increasingly sophisticated, in particular by their coming to incorporate representational models of the environment and important people in it and also of the self as a living active person.

The development during ontogeny of a set of systems of the kind described in humans, as well as in individuals of many other species, is attributed to the action of natural selection, namely to individuals well endowed with the potential to develop such systems having survived and bred more successfully than those less well endowed, in other words to Darwinian evolution. Since a disposition to show attachment behaviour in certain circumstances is regarded as an intrinsic part of human nature, reference to it as 'dependency' is not only misleading but seriously inappropriate because of the word's pejorative overtones.

Once attachment behaviour and other forms of biologically determined behaviour are conceived in terms of control theory, the problem of the purposiveness of behaviour is solved without abandoning the concept of causation. Furthermore the distinction between causation and function, sadly neglected in traditional psychoanalytic theory, becomes explicit. Activation, in which emotional arousal and expression play a critical part, and subsequently termination and change of emotional state are caused when a system constructed in a particular way receives information of particular sorts. Of the various consequences to which activation leads, the one postulated as its biological function is the one that, evidence suggests, has led to the system having evolved during phylogeny. In the case of attachment behaviour the function postulated is that of diminishing the risk of the individual coming to harm.

At this level of analysis the question of whether an individual is aware of what he is doing, let alone why he is doing it, has no relevance, in fact no more relevance than has the question of whether an individual is aware that he is breathing and, if so, realizes why he should be doing so. Biological systems serving vital functions, whether at a behavioural or a physiological level, must be capable of operating automatically. Nevertheless in the case of a human child awareness of what he is doing, and more particularly awareness of the conditions that will terminate his behaviour, soon emerges, certainly by the end of his first year, and is a factor of great importance. For, once it is clear that a child is aware of the conditions that will terminate his behaviour, we begin speaking of intention, of his desire to achieve a certain goal, of his being satisfied and happy when he does so and frustrated, anxious, or angry when he fails, of satisfaction bringing pleasure and frustration the reverse.

At this point I wish to emphasize the sharp distinction between conditions necessary to terminate a certain form of behaviour, commonly referred to as its goal, and the biological function the behaviour serves. In the case of attachment behaviour in childhood, whereas we commonly expect both mother and child to be aware of the conditions necessary to terminate it, for example, a certain degree of proximity, we do not expect awareness of function. The same holds in the case of eating and sexual behaviour. Most of us are aware that eating food will assuage our hunger and we find pleasure in eating; but only the sophisticated are concerned with its nutritional function. Similarly sexual desire can be assuaged without awareness of reproductive function. In both cases all but the sophisticated are concerned only with an urge to behave in a certain way and with the pleasure anticipated and received on reaching the terminating conditions (or goal), not with the biological function that the behaviour may serve. Often, in fact, when we feel emotionally impelled to act in a certain way that is readily explicable in terms of biological function, we concoct 'reasons' for doing so that bear little or no relation to the causes of our behaviour. For example, a child or adult, who in order to reduce risk is biologically disposed to respond to strange sounds in the dark by seeking his attachment figure, gives as his reason that he is afraid of ghosts. This is analogous to the 'reasons' for his behaviour concocted by someone who is, without knowing it, acting on a post-hypnotic suggestion.

The distinction I have drawn between the function served by a certain form of behaviour and our knowledge of, and our striving to reach, the conditions that will terminate that behaviour is one of the criteria that distinguish the biological realm from the psychological. Another is the distinction between, on the one hand, the behavioural system, postulated as a biological given, together with some (though not all) of the conditions that activate and terminate it, and, on the other, our awareness of the urge to reach a certain goal and our effort to find means to do so.

Earlier I remarked that, in understanding individual development, it is as necessary to consider the environment in which each individual develops as the genetic potentials with which he is endowed. The theoretical framework best suited to this purpose is that of developmental pathways proposed by the biologist, C.H. Waddington (1957).

Within this framework human personality is conceived as a structure that develops unceasingly along one or another of an array of possible and discrete pathways. All pathways are thought to start close together so that, at conception, an individual has access to a large range of pathways along any one of which he might travel. The one chosen, it is held, turns at each and every stage on an interaction between the organism as it has developed up to that moment and the environment in

64

which it then finds itself. Thus at conception development turns on interaction between the newly formed genome and the intrauterine environment; at birth it turns on interaction between the biological constitution of the neonate, including his germinal mental structure, and the family, or non-family, into which he is born; and at each age successively it turns on the personality structures then present and the family and later the wider social environment then current.

At conception the total array of pathways potentially open to an individual is determined by the make-up of the genome. As development proceeds and structures progressively differentiate, the number of pathways that remain open diminishes.

A principal variable in the development of each individual personality is, I believe, the pathway along which his attachment behaviour comes to be organized and further that that pathway is determined in high degree by the way his parent-figures treat him, not only during his infancy but throughout his childhood and adolescence as well. A principal means by which such experiences influence personality development is held to be through their effects on how a person construes the world about him and on how he expects persons to whom he might become attached to behave, both of which are derivatives of the representational models of his parents that he has built up during his childhood. Evidence suggests that these models tend to persist relatively unmodified at an unconscious level and to be far more accurate reflections of how his parents have really treated him than traditional opinion has supposed. Within this framework aberrations of behaviour and neurotic symptoms are conceived as due to the interactions that have occurred and that may still be occurring between an individual's personality as it has so far developed and the situation in which that individual now finds himself.

Let us pause here for a moment. In thus far sketching the conceptual framework I favour, I have doubtless said enough for you to see a number of points at which it differs from the traditional one. For example, the theory of motivation advanced differs radically from Freud's theory of psychic energy and drive, and the theory of developmental pathways differs in similar degree from his theories of libidinal phases, fixation, and regression. Furthermore the concept of attachment behaviour sees it as distinct from and of a status equal to that of eating and sexual behaviour, and as a characteristic present throughout life. Where lie the origins of these differences?

During the formative period of Freud's thought he was deeply interested in biology and concerned to formulate psychological theory in terms consistent with current biological thinking. This led him to explore the ideas of Darwin and other evolutionists of the period. At that time, the turn of the century, Darwin's theory of variation and natural selection as the agents of evolution was far from being the dominant theory it is today. On the contrary, Lamarck's theories regarding the inheritance of acquired characteristics and the influence that an animal's 'inner feeling of need' was thought to have on its structure were popular. So also was Haeckel's biogenetic law which, claiming that ontogeny recapitulates phylogeny, overlooks the fact that selection pressures operate at all phases of the life cycle and that new species often spring from the immature forms of earlier ones (neoteny). Freud, we know, was deeply influenced by both Lamarck and Haeckel and he commends their ideas repeatedly to his students.* The outcome was that much of his metapsychology and all his developmental psychology came to be founded on principles long since abandoned by biologists.

If, therefore, psychoanalysis is to become the natural science based on sound biological principles that Freud intended, there are compelling reasons for drastic changes in some at least of its basic assumptions. The framework I am advancing, based on neo-Darwinian principles and current work in developmental psychology and human information processing, is one such attempt.

Although psychoanalysis is avowedly a developmental discipline, it is nowhere weaker, I believe, than in its concepts of development. Many of the most influential of them, for

* For Freud's adherence to Lamarckian ideas see volume 3, chapter 10, of Ernest Jones's biography of Freud (Jones 1957). For the influence of Haeckel's biogenetic law see James Strachey's long editorial footnote to his translation of Freud's *Moses and Monotheism* (SE 23,102) and especially Frank Sulloway's enquiry into the origins of Freud's metapsychology (Sulloway 1979).

example, that of libidinal phases, stem straight from Haeckel. Thus in his *Introductory Lectures* of 1916–17, Freud emphasizes that the development of both ego and libido are to be understood as 'abbreviated recapitulations of the development which all mankind passed through from its primeval days' (Freud 1917, 354), whilst the development of the libido is also seen in terms of phylogeny and the various forms taken by the genital apparatus in animals. In a case study published about the same time, he attributes a person's ideas of 'observing parental intercourse, of being seduced in childhood and of being threatened with castration . . . [to] an inherited endowment, a phylogenetic heritage'; and he claims also that the Oedipus complex is among the 'phylogenetically inherited schemata' (Freud 1918, 97 and 119). All these ideas are repeated in his final work, e.g. Freud 1939, 99.

Now it may be that few analysts today would subscribe to Freud's original formulations; yet there can be no doubt of their pervasive influence not only on what is taught but on the prevailing assumptions of how our understanding of emotional and social development is best furthered. Thus pride of place continues to be given to reconstructions based on what is observed and inferred during treatment sessions, coupled with a persisting, if weakening, reluctance to give serious attention to the enormously important work now going on in the field of developmental psychology. Since in many previous publications I have drawn attention to the relevance of this work, I need say only that I believe all the developmental concepts of psychoanalysis will have to be re-examined, and that most of them will in due course be replaced by concepts now current among those who are studying the development of affectional bonds in infants and young children by means of direct observation. The understandable reserve with which many clinicians have viewed this type of work in the past would, I believe, be dispelled, were they to become familiar with the observations and ideas of such present leaders in the field as, for example, Mary Ainsworth (1977), John and Elizabeth Newson (Newson 1977), and Colwyn Trevarthen (1979).

Ignorant though many analytic theorists appear still to be of the value or even the very existence of these studies, there are, I

67

am glad to say, an increasing number of analytic therapists who draw on them in their treatment of patients. Let us turn therefore to the clinical field and consider the account given by a Californian analyst of his treatment of a woman patient, many of whose problems he attributes, I believe rightly, to events following her parents' divorce and the long period during her fifth and sixth years when she was in an institution. This account* not only illustrates the kinds of distressing personal problem to which experiences of these sorts give rise, including intense ambivalence, but serves also to pose questions of how issues of defence and affect are answered within the conceptual framework I am proposing.

The problems for which Mrs G came for analysis were that she felt irritable and depressed and filled, as she put it, with hate and evil. In addition she found herself frigid with her husband, emotionally detached, and wondering whether she was capable of loving anyone.

Mrs G had been 3 years old when her parents divorced. Her father left home and her mother, who began working long hours, had little time for her daughter. A year later, when Mrs G was 4, her mother placed her in an orphanage where she remained for eighteen long months. Thereafter, although she was back with her mother, family relationships continued to be disturbed and unhappy. As a result Mrs G left home during her teens and, before she was 21, had already been married and divorced twice. Her present husband was her third.

In the early phases of the analysis Mrs G was extremely reluctant to recall the painful events of her childhood; and when she did so she broke down into tears and sobbing. Nevertheless her analyst encouraged her to reflect on them further and to do so in minute detail since he believed this would help her. At the same time he paid at least equal attention to her relationship with himself in which, as would

* The account given here is derived from the contribution by Thomas Mintz to a symposium organized by the American Psychoanalytic Association on the effects on adults of object loss during the first five years of life (Mintz 1976).

be expected, all the interpersonal difficulties she had had in other close relationships recurred.

Amongst much else in her childhood that was painful, Mrs G recalled how sad she had felt on being parted from her pets when she was sent away to the orphanage. Sometimes she dreamed about her time there with feelings of being overwhelmed. She recalled feeling very small among the many children, how there were no toys, the harsh treatment meted out and how she had sometimes misbehaved deliberately in order to get smacked [which at least meant she was given some attention – J B].

After four years of analysis Mrs G's financial difficulties led to the decision to end treatment in six months' time. Inevitably the emotional conflicts she had in her relationship with her analyst became more acute. She now dreamed and day-dreamed more openly of him. From the first she had realized that parting would be painful. Separations had always made her angry and, as she put it now, 'anger makes me sad because it means the end. . . . I'm afraid you'll leave me or kick me out or put me away.' The analyst reminded her of how she had felt when sent to the orphanage. Struggling to think of herself as self-sufficient, she explained: 'I'm clinging on to me . . . I'm taking care of me all by myself.'

A few months later, as termination approached, she linked how she felt about her analyst with how she had felt earlier about her mother: 'I don't want to release my mother – I don't want to let her go – she's not going to get rid of me.' By this stage of her analysis her active yearning for love and care had returned together with her anger at those who had denied it her.

The radical change that had occurred in this woman was confirmed in other episodes. For example, during the early days of the analysis her cat had died but she had felt indifferent about it. As she had then explained: 'If I let it hurt me, I'd be saddened by everything. One will trigger off the rest.' But now, towards the end of the analysis, when another cat died, she wept.

Although therapy had restored this patient's feeling life and had resulted in her becoming able to make improved relationships, including that with her mother, a follow-up five years later showed, as would be expected, that she remained vulnerable to situations that arouse anxiety and sadness, such as separation and loss.

Let us examine the change that had occurred in this woman, whose condition might be described clinically as schizoid (Fairbairn 1940), or as false self (Winnicott 1960, 1974) or as narcissistic (Kohut 1971). Before the analysis she had felt emotionally detached and had wondered whether she was capable of loving anyone; a loss left her feeling indifferent. Now she had become aware how deeply she longed for love and care, and how angry she felt at not being given it; and a loss led to tears. Thus, in situations where they were missing before, responses laden with deep affect now appeared.

To account for such a change traditional explanations tend to use an hydraulic metaphor: affect has been dammed up and has now been discharged. The dam is regarded as a defence against an exessive quantity of excitation that is in danger of overwhelming the ego. Other explanations invoke processes postulated to occur in earliest infancy, for example, fixation in a phase of narcissism or a split in the ego resulting from the projection of a death instinct.

An explanation of this woman's condition that I believe to be much closer to our present knowledge of the early development of affectional bonds and consistent with what we know about human information processing runs as follows: as a result of the intense pain caused her during her early years by the prolonged and probably repeated frustration of her attachment behaviour, experienced as frustration of her urgent desire for love and care, the behavioural system(s) governing her attachment behaviour had become deactivated and had remained so despite her wishes to the contrary. As a result the desires, thoughts, and feeling that are part and parcel of attachment behaviour were absent from her awareness. The deactivation itself can be understood as due to the selective exclusion from processing of any information that, when processed, would lead to activation of the system.

The selective exclusion postulated, which, as recent experimental work shows, is well within the capabilities of our cognitive apparatus (Dixon 1971; Erdelyi 1974) and which I term defensive exclusion, requires constant cognitive activity at an unconscious level. The fact that the behavioural systems remain intact and capable in principle of being activated, and so may on occasion show brief or incipient activation, can account for all those phenomena that led Freud to his ideas about a dynamic unconscious and repression. In fact, the defensive exclusion that I postulate is no more than repression under another name, a name more in keeping with the conceptual framework adopted here.

The process of therapeutic change in this patient can then be understood as due to the patient, thanks to the relatively secure base provided by the analyst, developing sufficient courage to permit some of the information hitherto excluded to go forward for processing. This includes both information stemming from the present situation, for example, evidence of the analyst's genuine concern to help his patient and the conflicting thoughts, feelings, and behaviour that that arouses, and also information stored in memory, for example, memories of the very painful events of childhood and the thoughts, feelings, and behaviour aroused by them. As a rule information from the two sources is recovered as a chain in which information from the present, especially the transference, alternates with information from the past, with each link leading on to the next. Once the relevant information becomes accepted, of course, attachment behaviour is reactivated, together with the urges and desires, thoughts, and feeling that go with it. In traditional terms, the unconscious has been made conscious and the repressed urges and affects released.

Not infrequently, as with this patient, an analyst has the task of drawing a patient's attention to memories he believes of importance and encouraging her to reflect on them instead of turning her back on them. In doing this an analyst is guided, of course, by whatever theories of personality development and psychopathology he may espouse. This is a point at which analysts of different schools diverge. For some the events thought to be important might refer to feeding and weaning and fantasies about them during the earliest months of life; for others to toilet training or witnessing the primal scene during the second year; for others again to Oedipal situations and wishes during the third or fourth. In the case of Mrs G the analyst drew on his knowledge of responses of young children to events surrounding a prolonged separation from mother during several of the early years.

It is well recognized that not every child who has been in an institution for eighteen months during his fifth and sixth years develops psychologically along the kind of pathway followed by Mrs G. In her case other factors almost certainly entered in. In considering what they might have been, I am influenced by remarks Mrs G made during the final phases of the analysis, for example, her fear lest her analyst should 'kick her out' or 'put her away' and her memory of how determined she had been that her mother should not 'get rid' of her. This suggests that as a method of disciplining her daughter the mother may have repeatedly used threats to send her back to the institution, threats we know from other evidence are far from rare and that not only have a terrifying effect on a young child but are likely also to generate intense hatred in him. The better an analyst's knowledge of childhood conditions likely to lead to disturbed development, the better can he understand and help his patients.

Inevitably a patient's spontaneous or guided recollections of his childhood are of only suggestive value as evidence bearing on theories of personality development. What a patient tells us about his childhood and especially what an analyst subsequently reports his patient to have said are probably influenced as much or more by the analyst's preconceptions as by anything the patient may in fact have said or done; this is why I regard the systematic study by direct observation of children developing within different patterns of family care as indispensable for progress. Yet I also believe that observations made during therapy still have considerable research potential, although that potential will not be realized unless studies are conducted along far more systematic lines than have hitherto been usual and data obtained during therapy are constantly compared with data derived from other sources.

The research strength of the therapeutic situation lies not in what it tells us about the patient's past but in what it tells us about disturbances of personality functioning in the present, especially, I would claim, disturbances in a person's capacities to make secure attachments and the conditions in which these disturbances become ameliorated. The case of Mrs G can be used as an introduction to a research proposal, since there is much both in the personality disturbance she presents and in the course of her analysis that we have reason to believe are fairly typical.

Drawing on case reports already in the literature it would be possible to make a number of generalizations which could then be treated as predictions to be tested in further therapeutic work with patients showing similar clinical features. All such predictions, which would be conditional on the particular pattern of therapy to be followed,* could be couched in terms of what can be observed at first hand. They would include statements about how a patient would be expected to behave towards the analyst, the topics he would be expected to talk about or, in particular, avoid talking about, the affect he would be expected to show or not to show, and in what situations. Of special interest would be changes in behaviour, topic, and affect that would be expected to occur in relation to certain types of current event, both those occurring in the patient's everyday life and those occurring within the analysis. Events of the latter sort would include how the analyst behaves, what he says, and how he says it, with particular reference to interruptions in the analysis due to holidays, sickness, or other circumstances. Tape recording of sessions to avoid biased reporting would, of course, be necessary.

By following the procedures proposed it would be possible over a period of time to gather comparable bodies of data from two sources. One body of data would be gathered by means of direct observation of the development and patterning of affectional bonds during infancy and childhood in children experiencing different types of care. The other would be gathered, also by direct observation, of changes in the patterning of affectional

* The technique of analysis adopted by Mintz appears to have much in common with that adopted in the United Kingdom by Donald Winnicott; see the account by Guntrip (1975).

bonds during the course of a certain type of therapy. Provided that the conceptual frameworks used in making both sets of observations and the questions each set addresses are the same, findings could be compared and developmental hypotheses tested.

This is but one way in which psychoanalysis as a body of knowledge about personality development and psychopathology might move towards becoming the natural science Freud always intended it to be.

The conceptual framework sketched here serves, I believe, to accommodate a substantial proportion of the data that psycho-analysis has selected as within its domain and already guides productive research programmes (e.g. Parkes and Stevenson-Hinde 1982). The framework has the advantage of being com-patible with evolutionary biology and neurophysiology and promises greater economy and internal consistency than do traditional ones. Nevertheless what its strengths and weak-nesses will prove to be cannot be known without extensive testing of its powers to solve problems not yet studied, which include, for example, those of sexual development and devi-ation, and a far more intensive examination than has yet been possible of its usefulness in solving the problems already given attention.

Finally let us consider the issues raised by those who maintain that psychoanalysis is not and never can be a natural science. Their argument, we find, stems from the belief that scientific method is inseparable from logical positivism and reductionism. Although confidently and often dogmatically held earlier this century, this model of science is now discarded and its place taken by a philosophy of evolutionary epistemology (Popper 1972; Latakos 1974). This holds that all knowledge is conjectural and that science progresses through new theories coming to replace older ones when it becomes clear that a new theory is able to make sense of a greater circle of phenomena than are comprehended and explained by an older one and is able also to predict new phenomenena more accurately.* This same method

---

*The criterion of falsifiability on which Popper formerly laid great emphasis is no longer given so much prominence; though the constant comparison of theoretically derived predictions with an ever increasing array of observed data remains central.

is held to be applicable in all theoretical or generalizing sciences, whether they deal with physical, biological, or social phenomena. Furthermore, since to understand phenomena at any one level of complexity demands concepts appropriate to that level, the notion that complex phenomena must be explained in terms of concepts appropriate to a lower level of complexity, namely reductionism, is now recognized as fallacious. How these new ideas apply to our field is ably discussed by Holt (1981), Blight (1981), and Radford (1983).

Invaluable though scientific method is as a way of obtaining relatively reliable knowledge, resolving differences of opinion and making useful predictions, its limitations are nonetheless considerable. One is that science *deals in generalities but has little to say about singular specific events.* This is a vital distinction, as the physicist, Weisskopf (1981), points out. In the physical sciences it does not matter since physicists and engineers have no interest in the future of any particular atom or molecule. Once we move to the biological sciences, however, it does matter because biologists are frequently interested in individual organisms, all of which differ. In certain of the human sciences, moreover, the individual example is the very essence of the case. History, for instance, whether it deals with societies or persons or ideas, is always concerned with an appallingly complex sequence of highly specific interacting events which no amount of science can enable us to explain adequately, let alone predict. Thus the distinction between the natural sciences and the historical sciences is not that they use a different method of obtaining knowledge but that the problems that they strive to understand and the criteria they adopt are quite different. One is concerned to formulate general laws in terms of probabilities, the other to understand singular specific events in as much detail as possible. The distinction is central to the whole argument.

Under the label 'psychoanalysis', it is clear, two complementary disciplines are striving to live and develop. In so far as we are trying to understand the general principles accounting for personality development and psychopathology, necessary, for example, if we are to know what forms of child care tend to produce what sorts of personality formation, we adopt the criteria of the natural sciences. And we do the same when we

75

are trying to understand the essential features of effective therapy. In these fields we are dealing with statistical probabilities. In so far as we are concerned to understand the personal problems of a given individual and what events may have contributed to their development, necessary if we are to help him (though far from sufficient), we adopt the criteria of the historical sciences. Each approach contributes to our understanding; but, as I have pointed out in the previous lecture, only if we are clear-headed about what belongs to each, shall we be able to make progress.

LECTURE 5

Violence in the family

In the spring of 1983 I was invited to give the thirty-first annual Karen Horney Lecture by the Association for the Advancement of Psychoanalysis at the conference it was holding in New York City. A principal reason why I selected violence in the family as my theme was that research using the perspective of attachment theory was beginning to throw a shaft of light on a tragic but puzzling problem which, until recent years, had gone almost completely unrecognized by all those in the mental health field, not excluding myself.

Introduction

It seems to me that as psychoanalysts and psychotherapists we have been appallingly slow to wake up to the prevalence and far-reaching consequences of violent behaviour between members of a family, and especially the violence of parents. As a theme in the analytic literature and in training programmes it has been conspicuous by its absence. Yet there is now abundant evidence not only that it is much commoner than we had hitherto supposed but that it is a major contributory cause of a number of distressing and puzzling psychiatric syndromes. Since, moreover, violence breeds violence, violence in familes tends to perpetuate itself from one generation to the next.

Why family violence as a causal factor in psychiatry should

have been so neglected by clinicians – though, of course, not by social workers – would be a study in itself and cannot be entered on here. But the concentration in analytic circles on fantasy and the reluctance to examine the impact of real-life events has much to answer for. Ever since Freud made his famous, and in my view disastrous, volte-face in 1897, when he decided that the childhood seductions he had believed to be aetiologically important were nothing more than the products of his patients' imaginations, it has been extremely unfashionable to attribute psychopathology to real-life experiences. It is not an analyst's job, so the conventional wisdom has gone, to consider how a patient's parents may really have treated him, let alone to entertain the possibility, even probability, that a particular patient may have been the target for the violent words and violent deeds of one or both his parents. To focus attention on such possibilities, I have often been told, is to be seduced by our patients' prejudiced tales, to take sides, to make scapegoats of perfectly decent parents. And in any case, it is asserted, to do so could be of no help to the patient, would in fact be anti-therapeutic. It was indeed largely because the adverse behaviour of parents towards their children was such a taboo subject in analytic circles when I was starting my professional work that I decided to focus my research on the effects on children of real-life events of another sort, namely separation and loss.

Of course, Karen Horney, in whose honour we are meeting today, did not share those prejudices. On the contrary, she is quite explicit in attributing many of her patients' problems to the adverse influences they had met with as children. As she writes in the opening pages of her book, *Neurosis and Human Growth* (1951), these adverse influences 'boil down to the fact that the people in the environment are too wrapped up in their own neuroses to be able to love the child, or even to conceive of him as the particular individual he is . . .'; and she goes on to list some of the many ways in which, unfortunately, parents can exert a harmful influence on their children. But I know well that these views were not always well received by her colleagues.

Today the scene is changing – though still far too slowly. For example, no one with eyes to see can any longer doubt that all too many children are battered by their parents, either verbally or physically or both, nor that all too many women are battered by husband or boy-friend. Moreover, our horror that parents can behave so is nowadays mitigated by our increasing knowledge of the kind of childhoods these parents have themselves had. Whilst horror at their acts is inevitable, greater understanding of how they have come to behave in these violent ways evokes compassion rather than blame. So far from wishing to scapegoat parents we wish to help them. So far from refusing to see that parents sometimes engage in horrific behaviour, we seek ways to succour the casualties, old as well as young, psychological as well as physical. Above all we seek ways of preventing violent patterns developing in new families. Let us hope that the policy of head-in-sand has had its day.

Conceptual framework

In seeking to understand the more extreme examples of violence in the family it is useful to consider first what we know about the more moderate and everyday example of members of a family getting angry with each other. Young children – and often older ones too – are commonly jealous of the attention mother gives the new baby. Lovers quarrel when one thinks the other is looking elsewhere – and the same is true after marriage. Moreover a woman may get very angry with her child if he does something dangerous, like running into the roadway, and also with her husband if he risks life or limb by taking unnecessary risks. Thus we take it for granted that, when a relationship to a special loved person is endangered, we are not only anxious but are usually angry as well. As responses to the risk of loss, anxiety and anger go hand in hand. It is not for nothing that they have the same etymological root.

In the situations described anger is often functional. When child or spouse behaves dangerously, an angry protest is likely to deter. When a lover's partner strays, a sharp reminder of how much he or she cares may work wonders. When a child finds himself relatively neglected in favour of the new baby, assertion of his claims may redress the balance. Thus in the right place, at the right time, and in right degree, anger is not only appropriate but may be indispensable. It serves to deter from dangerous behaviour, to drive off a rival, or to coerce a partner. In each case the aim of the angry behaviour is the same – to protect a relationship which is of very special value to the angry person.

This being so, it is necessary to be clear why certain specific relationships, often called libidinal relationships, should become so very important in the lives of each one of us.

In his attempts to solve this problem Freud looked to the physics and biology of his day. Libidinal relationships, he proposed, were consequent on the individual's needs for food and sex. Subsequently, to account for some of the more puzzling manifestations of anger, he stepped outside biology to propose a death instinct. These hypotheses, framed in terms of the accumulation and discharge of psychic energies, led to a metapsychology so remote from clinical observation and experience that a great many analytically oriented clinicians have, implicitly or explicitly, abandoned it. To the resulting vacuum one reaction has been the development of a school of thought that has decided not only to divorce psychoanalysis from biology but to dispense altogether with scientific method and instead to espouse hermeneutics. Another and opposite reaction has been to explore the principles found useful in modern biology, principles totally different from those of Freud's day, to see whether they are more in tune with our clinical observations and might therefore be used to construct a new metapsychology, or conceptual framework as it would now be called. That is the course that I and a number of others are following.

The specific relationships, threats to which may arouse anger, are of three main types: relationships with a sexual partner (boy-friend, girl-friend, or spouse), relationships with parents, and relationships with offspring. Each type of relationship is shot through with strong emotion. In high degree indeed, a person's whole emotional life – the underlying tone of how he feels – is determined by the state of these long-term, committed relationships. As long as they are running smoothly he is content; when they are threatened he is anxious and perhaps angry; when he has endangered them by his own actions he feels guilty; when they are broken he feels sad; and when they are resumed he is joyful.

In helping us understand why the state of these relationships should have such a profound effect on a person's feeling life two branches of modern biology – ethology and evolution theory – are extremely illuminating. Not only do all three of the relationships in question have counterparts in a wide range of other species but all three are intimately concerned with the vital biological functions of reproduction and, especially, the survival of young. It is therefore more than likely that a human being's powerful propensity to make these deep and long-term relationships is the result of a strong gene-determined bias to do so, a bias that has been selected during the course of evolution. Within this frame of reference a child's strong propensity to attach himself to his mother and his father, or to whomever else may be caring for him, can be understood as having the function of reducing the risk of his coming to harm. For to stay in close proximity to, or in easy communication with, someone likely to protect you is the best of all possible insurance policies. Similarly a parent's concern to care for his or her offspring plainly has the function of contributing to the child's survival. That success in the maintenance of these long-term relationships should usually bring satisfaction and contentment, and that failure should bring frustration, anxiety, and sometimes despair are, on this reading, the prizes and penalties selected during evolution to guide us in our activities.

It is within this evolutionary perspective that I believe we can understand how angry behaviour between members of a family can often be functional. For, as I said earlier, in the right place, at the right time, and in right degree, anger can serve to maintain these vitally important long-term relationships. But, as is very obvious, anger can be overdone. My thesis is simply that a great deal of the maladaptive violence met with in families can be understood as the distorted and exaggerated versions of behaviour that is potentially functional, especially attachment behaviour on the one hand and caregiving behaviour on the other.

There is now a considerable literature on the nature of the child's tie to his mother, traditionally referred to as dependency and now conceived in terms of attachment and careseeking. But in general terms, attachment behaviour results in one individual, usually the one who is less able to cope, maintaining proximity to, and/or communication with, another individual, seen as better able to cope. This behaviour is elicited especially by pain, fatigue, or anything frightening, and also by the caregiver being or appearing to be, inaccessible. Although conceived as being in part preprogrammed, there is now abundant evidence that the particular pattern in which attachment behaviour becomes organized during development is much influenced by how it is responded to by a child's principal caregivers, in the huge majority of cases his mother and father. Briefly, it seems clear that sensitive loving care results in a child developing confidence that others will be helpful when appealed to, becoming increasingly self-reliant and bold in his explorations of the world, co-operative with others, and also – a very important point – sympathetic and helpful to others in distress. Conversely, when a child's attachment behaviour is responded to tardily and unwillingly and is regarded as a nuisance, he is likely to become anxiously attached, that is, apprehensive lest his caregiver be missing or unhelpful when he needs her and therefore reluctant to leave her side, unwillingly and anxiously obedient, and unconcerned about the troubles of others. Should his caregivers, in addition, actively reject him, he is likely to develop a pattern of behaviour in which avoidance of them competes with his desire for proximity and care, and in which angry behaviour is apt to become prominent. I shall say more about this later.

One further point about attachment behaviour I wish to emphasize is that it is a characteristic of human nature throughout our lives – from the cradle to the grave. Admittedly it is usually less intense and less demanding in adolescents and adults than it is in earlier years. Yet an urgent desire for love and care is natural enough when a person is anxious or distressed. It is therefore most unfortunate that, due to misleading theory, the pejorative adjectives 'infantile' and 'regressive' are now so widely current in clinical circles. They are words I never use.

Whilst the systematic study of attachment behaviour, and especially the conditions influencing how it develops, has been in progress for twenty years, the systematic study of caregiving, or parenting, and how it develops is only in its beginnings. The approach I regard as the most promising is again an ethological one. This assumes that in humans as well as in other species parenting behaviour, like attachment behaviour, is in some degree preprogrammed and therefore ready to develop along certain lines when conditions elicit it. This means that in the ordinary course of events the parent of a baby experiences a strong urge to behave in certain typical sorts of way, for example, to cradle the infant, to soothe him when he cries, to keep him warm, protected, and fed. Such a viewpoint, of course, does not imply that the appropriate behaviour patterns manifest themselves complete in every detail from the first. Clearly that is not so, neither in man nor in any other mammalian species. All the detail is learned, some of it during interaction with babies and children, much of it through observation of how other parents behave, starting during the parent-to-be's own childhood and the way his parents treated him and his siblings.

Research findings

In considering what is now known of the individuals involved in family violence, and the circumstances in which it takes place, I start with women who physically assault their children and, next, with the effects on the children of such assaults. My reason for doing so is that in these two areas the research findings seem most adequate. And in the light of those findings we can proceed to consider what is known about men who batter wives or children, a problem area just as important but at present less well researched.

The findings of the many studies of women known to have battered their children show considerable agreement (see review by Spinetta and Rigler 1972). Though probably commoner among families of lower socio-economic status, child abuse occurs also in middle-class families where it is likely to be hidden behind a façade of ultra-respectability.

On the surface abusing individuals vary from being cold, rigid, obsessional, and censorious to being passive, unhappy, and disorganized. Yet emotionally they have much in common. Among features reported as especially frequent among abusive mothers we find the following: prone to periods of intense anxiety punctuated by outbursts of violent anger, they are said to be impulsive and 'immature'. Although their 'dependency needs' are described as exceptionally strong, they are extremely distrustful and consequently unable or unwilling to make close relationships. Socially they are isolated. Having no one else to turn to, many of them seek care and comfort from one of their own children whom they treat as though they were much older than they are (Morris and Gould 1963).

As regards childhood experience many researchers have noted that most of such women have had a miserable childhood and, as one pair of researchers put it, 'have been deprived of basic mothering' (Steele and Pollock 1968). An appreciable minority were themselves battered as children.*

To anyone thinking in terms of attachment theory the notion at once suggests itself that these woman are suffering from an extreme degree of anxious attachment and consequently that experiences of long or repeated separations and/or of being repeatedly threatened with abandonment would be a common feature of their childhoods. In a relatively small study these hypotheses have now been tested by Pauline DeLozier (1982), working in Los Angeles. Her samples consisted of eighteen working-class women known to have assaulted their children physically and eighteen others from the same socio-economic class, and matched for age (most in their thirties) and number of children, who had not done so. All subjects were given a semi-structured interview and a questionnaire to complete and were tested on the Hansburg Separation Anxiety Test (Hansburg 1972). In the latter a series of pictures depicting scenes either of a child leaving his parents or of parents leaving the child is shown and the subject invited to describe what she would feel and do in the situation concerned.

---

* In a study by Baldwin (1977) of thirty-eight children who had been physically abused to an exceptionally severe degree, two-fifths of the parents had suffered physical abuse as children and more than half severe or prolonged mental abuse. Baldwin calls attention to the marked tendency of many of these parents, when interviewed, to make broad generalizations about their childhood in which an idealized picture is presented, a picture that stands in stark contrast to the grim episodes described when detailed questions are asked. In this field inexperienced clinicians and interviewers are likely to be gravely misled.

The results of the Separation Anxiety Test showed, as expected, that most of the abusing mothers were extremely sensitive to any type of separation situation, even the most everyday and commonplace, with responses indicative of high levels of anxiety and/or anger. The responses showed, in addition, that, while these women yearned for care, all they expected was rejection. Supporting another of the initial hypotheses was a high incidence of responses indicating anxious concern for the welfare of parents. For all these features the incidences in the control group, although not negligible, were significantly lower. For example, whereas twelve of the eighteen abusing mothers were rated as showing the highest degree of anxious attachment, only two of the control group were so rated.

As regards the childhood experiences of these women, the results, as reported in interview and qiestionnaire, supported some of the initial hypotheses but did not support others. For example, in view of previous reports DeLozier had expected to find a significantly higher incidence of separations from parents in the childhoods of the abusive mothers but this was not found. By contrast, her expectation that a high proportion of these women would have experienced their parents as having repeatedly threatened to abandon them was fulfilled, a finding in keeping with the view that repeated threats to abandon are as pathogenic as actual separations and probably more so (Bowlby 1973). In a similiar way, although actual violence from a parent had apparently not been common, many of the abusing mothers had suffered repeated threats of being beaten, maimed, or even killed.

Another striking feature of the childhoods of the abusing mothers, also in keeping with expectations, was that only a minority of them (seven) had felt they could turn to mother for help when in distress. Amongst those who could not were some who described someone else, a relative or neighbour, who would have been helpful; but four of the eighteen had known of absolutely no one. Amongst the controls, by contrast, all but three had felt they could turn to mother, and each of the others had at least known of someone else.

Thus, unlike a girl who grows up in an ordinary reasonably happy home who can rely on her mother in an emergency, a

85

majority of these women could never do so. Indeed, and again as predicted, for many of them the relationship of daughter to mother had been reversed and it was they who had been expected to care for the parent.*

Given the childhood experiences these women had had, it is not difficult to understand why they had grown up as they had. Threats to abandon a child make her (or him) intensely anxious about any separation, however routine it might appear to others, and also intensely angry with her parent for threatening her so. Moreover failures to respond helpfully when a child is in distress, combined with repeated and impatient rejections, lead her to be deeply suspicious of everyone else. Thus, whilst constantly yearning for the love and care she has never had, she has no confidence she will ever receive it; and she will mistrust any offer she may receive. Small wonder therefore, if when a woman with this background becomes a mother, that there are times when, instead of being ready to mother her child, she looks to her child to mother her. Small wonder too if when her child fails to oblige and starts crying, demanding care and attention, that she gets impatient and angry with it.

It is against this background, I believe, that a mother's violent assaults on a child can be understood. Although I have never treated a woman who actually assaulted her child physically, I have treated one who came perilously close to doing so.

The reason I began seeing this woman, whom I will call Mrs Q, was that the doctor at the well-baby clinic she attended was concerned about her son, aged 18 months; he was refusing to eat and was losing weight. When I saw them both, it was at once apparent that Mrs Q was intensely anxious and depressed and had been so since the boy's birth. On enquiry I found that she was terrified lest her son die and was therefore pestering him to eat. She also told me that she had sometimes had impulses to throw the baby out of the window. Only much later did she tell me that on occasion she became hysterical, smashed the dishes, and battered the baby's pram. She was intensely anxious talking

---

* DeLozier's study has now been repeated by Mitchell (in preparation) on samples of Mexican–American mothers with closely similar results.

to me and fully expected me to turn on her angrily. On my suggestion she came to see me for psychotherapy once a week.

The picture she gave me of her childhood, told reluctantly in fragments but always consistently, was one I now know to be typical. She recalled bitter quarrels between her parents in which they assaulted one another and threatened murder, and how her mother would repeatedly bring pressure on the family by threatening to desert. On two occasions Mrs Q had returned from school to find her mother with her head in the gas oven, and at other times her mother would pretend to have deserted by disappearing for half a day. Naturally Mrs Q grew up terrified that if she did anything wrong her mother would go. Moreover things were made even worse by her mother insisting that she breathe not a word about these terrifying events to anyone outside the home.

Mrs Q, who had been a skilled technician before marriage, was known as a very helpful neighbour and did all she could to be a good wife and mother – in which for the most part she succeeded. Yet she was subject to these violent and destructive outbursts which frightened and puzzled her and about which she felt intense shame.

After some time I had little doubt that the angry outbursts were to be understood as the expression of intense anger which, generated initially and over many years by her mother's repeated threats to abandon the family, had early in her life become directed away from her mother and towards less dangerous targets. Terrified then and later of ever expressing her anger directly, she redirected* it towards something which, or someone who, could not retaliate. As a child, Mrs Q recalled, she had sometimes retreated to her room and attacked her dolls. Now it was her crockery, the pram, and almost but not quite the baby. Each current outburst, I suspected, was triggered by her mother who, dominating and interfering as ever, still visited her daughter every day.

* Because it is less ambiguous, I find the ethologist's term 'redirection' preferable to its clinical equivalent 'displacement'. The redirection of hostile behaviour away from a more dominant animal is well known in other species.

This explanation fits what facts we have and has the merit, not always appreciated in clinical circles, of being simple. Not surprisingly, other workers in the field have also proposed it (e.g. Feinstein, Paul, and Pettison 1964). In other cases, it is clear, a husband has violently abused his wife and she, violently angry in return, has redirected it against their child.

In turning next to the effects on the personality development of children who are assaulted, we have to bear in mind that the physical assaults are not the only episodes of hostility from parents that these children have experienced. In very many cases indeed the physical assaults are but the tip of an iceberg – the manifest signs of what have been repeated episodes of angry rejection, verbal as well as physical. In most cases therefore the psychological effects can be regarded as the outcome of prolonged hostile rejection and neglect. Nevertheless the experiences of individual children can vary greatly. A few, for example, may receive reasonably good care and only very occasionally suffer an outburst of parental violence. For these reasons it is no surprise that the socio-emotional development of the children varies also. Here I describe findings that appear to be fairly typical.

Those who have observed such children in their homes or elsewhere describe them variously as depressed, passive, and inhibited, as 'dependent' and anxious, and also as angry and aggressive (Martin and Rodeheffer 1980). Gaensbauer and Sands (1979), in endorsing this picture, emphasize how disturbing to a caregiver such behaviour can be. The children fail to participate in play and show little or no enjoyment. Expression of feeling is often so low key that it is easy to overlook, or else is ambiguous and contrary. Crying may be prolonged and unresponsive to comforting; anger is easily aroused, intense, and not readily resolved. Once established, these patterns tend to persist.

An issue much discussed in the literature is the degree to which an infant's prematurity, ill-health, or difficult temperament may have contributed to a mother's problems and so ultimately to its having been ill-treated. In some cases these factors play a part, but they do so only when a mother reacts

unfavourably to the baby and thereby sets up a vicious circle.*
Such a sequence, of course, is all too likely to occur when a
mother has herself had a difficult childhood, has grown up
emotionally disturbed, and has little or no emotional support or
help after her baby is born.

Towards his or her parent an abused toddler often shows a
striking picture of frozen watchfulness, hyper-alert for what
might happen. But some show also an unusual sensitivity to the
needs of their parents (Malone 1966). There are, in fact, good
reasons for thinking that some children learn early that it is
possible to placate a disturbed and potentially violent mother by
constant attention to her wishes.**

In a nursery setting battered infants and toddlers have a
reputation for finding it difficult to make relationships, either
with caregivers or with other children, and also for being very
aggressive. In recent years these observations have been confirmed and extended by more systematic research which has
focused attention both on the particular patterns of behaviour
shown and on details of the situations in which each occurs.
The findings that follow stem from a study being conducted at
Berkeley by Main and George (George and Main 1979; Main and
George 1985).

Their aim was to compare the behaviour in a day-nursery
setting of two groups of children in the age-range 1 to 3 years.
One group of ten were known to have been physically assaulted
by a parent. The other group of ten were matched for all relevant
variables but had not been assaulted; they were, however, in
nurseries set up to care for children from families known to
be under stress. To obtain data each child was observed for
four periods each of thirty minutes on four different days

* There is now good evidence that, given sensitive mothering, difficult
infants develop favourably, with only few exceptions (Sameroff and
Chandler 1975) and, conversely, that a potentially easy baby is likely to
develop unfavourably if given insensitive care (Sroufe 1983).

** I am indebted for this point to Pat Crittenden (personal communication)
who has observed such apparently placatory behaviour in young abused
children, some less than two years old. Similar behaviour has been observed also in young children whose mothers are seriously depressed
(Pound, 1982).

spread over three weeks. Observers were instructed to record all socially relevant behaviour, including such small movements as head-turning or stepping backwards.

In analysing the data, the children's social behaviour was divided into four categories: approach, avoidance, approach-avoid, and aggression. It was also divided according to whom the behaviour was directed – another child or a caregiver. Another distinction was between behaviour initiated by the observed child and behaviour which occurred in response to a friendly approach by another child or adult. Results are expressed in terms of the mean number of incidents of a particular type of behaviour of the children in each group or else of the number of children in each group who showed that type of behaviour.

As regards occasions when a child initiated social contact, either with another child or a caregiver, no appreciable differences were observed between the children in each group. By contrast, very striking differences were observed in the ways the children responded to a friendly approach from the other. Characteristic responses of the abused children were either to take straight avoiding action or else to show *both* approach *and* avoidance behaviour, either in quick succession or in some combination of the two. Examples are: 'she creeps towards him but suddenly veers away', and 'she crawls towards the caregiver but with head averted'. Thus, when the overtures come from a caregiver, the abused toddlers were three times more likely than the controls to take avoiding action; whilst seven of them, compared to only one, showed the curious combination of alternation of approach and avoidance. When the overtures came from other children, the differences were even more marked. For example, whereas none of the controls showed approach-avoidance, all ten of the abused toddlers did so.

Aggressive behaviour was fairly common in both groups of toddlers, though, as predicted, it was significantly more so in the abused group. Not only did the abused toddlers assault other children twice as often as the controls, but five of them assaulted or threatened to assault an adult, behaviour seen in none of the controls. In addition the abused toddlers were notable for a particularly disagreeable type of aggression, termed

90

'harassment' (Manning, Heron, and Marshall 1978). This consists of malicious behaviour which appears to have the sole intent of making the victim show distress. Almost always it occurs suddenly without any evident cause and so contrasts with hostility which occurs in reaction to a provocation. Such attacks, coming unpredictably out of the blue, are frightening and invite retaliation. Clinical studies, referred to later, report them to be directed especially towards an adult to whom the child is becoming attached.

In view of the behaviour so far described it is not surprising to find that abused toddlers are singularly unsympathetic to age-mates in distress. The studies of Zahn-Waxler and Radke-Yarrow have shown that infants and pre-school children who have affectionate and caring parents commonly express concern when another child is distressed and often make moves to comfort him or her (Zahn-Waxler, Radke-Yarrow, and King 1979). This type of behaviour was also seen at least once in five of the control children in the Main and George study; but on no occasion did any of the abused toddlers show the slightest hint of it. Instead, and unlike the controls, they reacted with some combination of fear, distress, or anger; and three behaved hostilely to the crying child. For example, one small boy of 2 years 8 months slapped a little girl who was crying, exclaiming repeatedly 'Cut it out, cut it out'. He proceeded then to pat her back and next to hiss at her with bared teeth; before anyone could intervene, his patting had turned to beating.

My reasons for giving so much attention to these observations of young children will, I am sure, be apparent. They show with unmistakable clarity how early in life certain characteristic patterns of social behaviour – some hopeful for the future, others ominous – become established. They leave no doubts either about what types of family experience influence development in one direction or another. Again and again we see details in the behaviour of a toddler, or in what he says, that are plainly straight replicas of how that toddler has himself been treated. Indeed the tendency to treat others in the same way that we ourselves have been treated is deep in human nature; and at no time is it more evident than in the earliest years. All parents please note!

Firm evidence of how these children develop must await an appropriately designed longitudinal study. There is evidence that, if conditions of care improve, some recover sufficiently to pass for normal (Lynch and Roberts. 1982); others do not. Some have suffered serious brain damage and become diagnosed as mentally handicapped (e.g. Martin and Rodeheffer 1980). For many others adverse conditions of care continue. Furthermore, once a child has developed the types of disagreeable behaviour described, it is not easy for an adult, whether parent, foster-parent, or professional, to give him the continuous affectionate care he needs, whilst treating such children by psychotherapy is extremely taxing. The sudden unprovoked attacks, which in older children can easily be damaging, are especially hard to take.

Some of these emotionally disturbed children, we know, reach psychiatric clinics where the origin of their condition, I suspect, more often than not goes unrecognized. Amongst those who have treated these children, some of them psychotic, and who have traced the source of their troubles are Stroh (1974), Bloch (1978), and Hopkins (1984). Each notes the extreme degree of ambivalence to be expected: one moment the child is hugging the therapist, the next he is kicking her. During adolescence and early adult life, some, mostly male, become diagnosed as aggressive psychopaths and/or violent delinquents (e.g. Farrington 1978). Others, especially females perhaps, are found to be suffering from multiple personality (Bliss 1980). Once psychiatrists become aware of the profound and far-reaching effects of childhood abuse and rejection, and the extent to which relevant information is suppressed and falsified by parents and overlooked by clinicians, many more cases are sure to be identified.

A significant proportion of rejected and abused children grow up to perpetuate the cycle of family violence by continuing to respond in social situations with the very same patterns of behaviour that they had developed during early childhood.

A type of response found to be characteristic of many abusive parents, and of a kind which we have already seen to be charac-teristic of abused toddlers, is reported, for example, by Frodi and Lamb (1980). In a laboratory study, in which videotapes of crying infants were shown, abusive mothers were found to respond to a crying infant with less sympathy than did a group of non-abusive mothers and also with more annoyance and anger. Furthermore these same adverse responses were shown by the abusive mothers even when they were shown video tapes of smiling infants, which suggested they disliked any form of interaction with an infant.

Let us turn now, rather belatedly, to the behaviour of men who ill-treat girl-friend or wife.

Two of my social work colleagues at the Tavistock, Janet Mattinson and Ian Sinclair (1979), describe a man, Mr S, who was apt, inexplicably and unpredictably, to attack his wife. At the time when he asked for an interview his wife had recently left him; she had just had their first baby. Although hesitant at first, Mr S fairly soon began telling the social worker how much he feared his own violence. He loved his wife, he said, and felt his violent behaviour to be quite unwarranted, akin to madness. Subsequently, speaking of his childhood, he described how he had been a member of a large working-class family in which he had received little more than harsh and unsympathetic treatment. His parents, he said, were constantly engaged in violent quarrels. Exploring in later interviews how he had felt as a child, struggling for the love he never got, he was struck by the suggestion that it was probably a mixture of anger and despair. This made sense to him, he said: it relieved him of his fear that his violence was inexplicable. The outbreaks that had led to his wife's departure, it was noted, had occurred soon after the baby's birth. Since we know from other studies, e.g. Marsden and Owens (1975), that intense jealousy of a wife's attention to the children is a common precipitant of a husband's violence, Mr S's outbursts were in all likelihood triggered by the baby's arrival.

Sudden and on the surface inexplicable outbursts of violence, similar to those of Mr S, are found to be characteristic of a significant proportion of men who batter wives; for example, they occurred in five out of the nineteen cases investigated by Marsden and Owens (1975). The hypothesis that most of such

men are ill-treated and battered children now grown up is supported by several findings. In one study (Gayford 1975) information from the wives was that fifty-one out of a hundred violent
men had themselves been battered as children. Moreover thirty-
three of the hundred had already been convicted of other violent
offences and, as already noted, studies show that most violent
offenders come from homes in which they were subjected to
cruel and brutal treatment (Farrington 1978).

Finally we find that many of the wives who are battered have
come from disturbed and rejecting homes, in which a significant
minority were themselves battered as children (Gayford 1975).
These experiences had led them to leave home in their teens, to
link up with almost the first man they met, all too often from a
similar background, and quickly to become pregnant. For the
unprepared and anxiously attached girl, having to care for a
baby creates a thousand problems; moreover her attention to the
baby provokes intense jealousy in her partner. These are some
of the processes by which an inter-generational cycle of violence
becomes perpetuated.

Let us return now to the study of Mattinson and Sinclair
(1979) who describe patterns of interaction that they found were
common in certain families.

The interviews with Mr S were part of a study undertaken in
order to find out more of what is happening in the kind of
intensely disturbed family that creates endless problems for the
medical and social services and which is known to be extra-
ordinarily difficult to help. In these families, it seemed, violence
or threats of violence occurred almost daily. Time and again the
couple had separated only to come together again after a few
days or weeks. Sometimes, after hard words from his wife, a
husband would go off on his own, only to hive back again a
short time later. Or a wife, physically assaulted by her husband,
would leave with the children but return within days to the very
same situation. What seemed so extraordinary to the workers
was the length of time some of these marriages had lasted.
One question they asked themselves therefore was what was
keeping the partners together.

What they found was that, whilst the violence of a husband
and the angry threatening remarks of a wife seemed to dominate

the scene, each partner was deeply, if anxiously, attached to the other and had developed a strategy designed to control the other and to keep him or her from departing. Various techniques were in use, mainly coercive, and many of them of a kind that to an outsider would appear not only extreme but counterproductive. For example, threats to desert or to commit suicide were common, and suicidal gestures not infrequent. These were usually effective in the short term by ensuring the partner's concerned attention, though they also aroused his or her guilt and anger. Most of the suicide attempts, it was found, were reactions to specific events, particularly desertions either actual or threatened.

A coercive technique, used especially by the men, was to 'imprison' the wife by such means as locking her in the house, or padlocking her clothes, or else retaining all the money and doing the shopping so as to prevent her from seeing anyone else. The intensely ambivalent attachment of one man who adopted this technique was such that he not only locked his wife in but he also locked her out. He would throw her out of the house telling her never to return but, after she had got to the street, would run after her and pull her back to their flat.

A third coercive technique was battering. As one man put it, in his family asking for something was always done with fists. No wife enjoyed this treatment, but some got a wry satisfaction from it. For example, one woman, when explaining why she did not wish for a separation, announced with a note of triumph in her voice that her husband had threatened he would come to 'get her' if she moved out. He needed her too, she insisted. In most of these marriages, it was found, each party was apt to stress how much the other needed them, whilst disclaiming their own need for the partner. By need, of course, they meant what I am calling their desire for a caregiving figure. What they dreaded most was loneliness.

Preventive measures

This ends my description of the problems met with in violent families and the theoretical perspective in which I believe it useful to approach them. What actions then are called for?

95

Much skilled and devoted work has gone into helping families in which abuse has already occurred, and much thought given to problems of management (Helfer and Kempe, 1976; Lynch and Roberts 1982). Since every study has shown how very difficult and time-consuming all such work is, we ask about prospects for prevention. Here lies hope. In what follows I describe a type of service which has been pioneered in the United Kingdom and which is now spreading steadily with encouragement from government. No doubt similar services are to be found in various parts of the United States also, but naturally I know less about them.

The service pattern which is so promising, at least for some families, is one known as Home-Start (which was begun in Leicester) (Harrison 1981).* It is an independently organized home-visiting scheme which offers support, friendship, and practical assistance to young families experiencing difficulties. It is staffed by volunteers who work in close liaison with the related statutory services and who also receive support and guidance from a professional. All visits are by invitation of the family and on their terms. There are no contracts and no time limits.

Each volunteer is a mother who undertakes to make regular visits to one or, at most, two families with the aim of establishing a relationship in which time and understanding can be shared. Every effort is made to encourage the parents' strengths and to reassure them that difficulties in caring for children are not unusual, and also that it is possible for family life to be enjoyable. New volunteers, who are mainly between the ages of 30 and 45, attend a preparatory course, one day a week for ten weeks, and receive regular ongoing training afterwards.

There are many advantages in the visitors being volunteers. First a volunteer has *time*: in practice it was found in the pioneer scheme that the average time each volunteer was spending with her family in its own home was six hours a week. Secondly she meets the mother on a level of equality and feels free to contribute to household activities in any way that seems appropriate. Thirdly

* Another initiative, serving a severely deprived area in inner London and known as Newpin, is also promising (Pound and Mills 1985).

she can compare notes and talk about experiences with her own children. Fourthly, and very important, she can sometimes make herself available to be contacted during an evening or at a weekend.

The families visited are, of course, ones in which difficulties are either already present or appear imminent. Since the service is not aimed specifically at abusing families, a family participating need not feel labelled in any way. Nevertheless the service deals with a fair number of families who have one or more children on a register of children at risk of abuse. In the first eight years of the pioneer scheme no less than a quarter of the families visited were in that category.

Often visiting is started whilst a mother is still pregnant. Most of those visited are young, impulsive, and dreadfully isolated and have never experienced affection, care, or security. In such cases the principal role of the volunteer is to mother the mother and so, by example, to encourage her to mother her own child. She will also talk and play with the children, again providing the mother with an example she has never had. Perhaps later, once confidence has grown, the volunteer may assist by helping the mother acquire basic household skills she has never learned. The key to the relationship is that the volunteer is herself a mother who knows all the problems from the inside.

There are many cases which are recognized to be unsuited for inclusion in a service of this sort.* For those suitable the degree of success reported is most encouraging, as shown by an evaluation of the first four years' work of the pioneer service, carried out by an independent researcher whose monograph (van der Eyken 1982) gives a full account of the project. Taking a random sample of one in five of the 288 families visited, he asked those concerned how they assessed the outcome at the end of the volunteer's visiting, using a three-point scale: no change, some change, considerable change. The results showed that the volunteers were the most pessimistic, rating only half the families

* Harrison (1981) lists the following: where a parent is known to be chronically ill mentally, is suffering from a serious degenerative illness, is a recidivist, or is intent on the children being admitted to care. Also excluded are families in which the children are at risk of abuse by a mother's cohabitee.

as showing considerable change and one in ten as failures. The social workers who had referred cases were more hopeful, rating rather more than half as showing considerable change and the remainder as showing at least some. Those most enthusiastic for the work were the health visitors (public health nurses) and the families themselves. Of the fifty-eight families who assessed themselves, forty-seven (85 per cent) claimed a considerable change had occurred, six claimed some change and only two believed there had been none.

In a field that is both deeply troubling and notoriously difficult these findings give hope.

On knowing what you are not supposed to know and feeling what you are not supposed to feel

Early in 1979 I was invited to contribute to a special number of the Canadian Journal of Psychiatry *to honour Emeritus Professor Eric Wittkower who had held a chair of psychiatry at McGill University in Montreal from 1952 to 1964 and was then celebrating his eightieth birthday. This I was very glad to do. The resulting paper, with the above title, also formed the basis of lectures that I gave on various occasions during subsequent years. On one such occasion, in Rome, I met with two cognitive therapists, Giovanni Liotti and Vittorio Guidano, and was surprised and delighted to find how much we had in common. One consequence of our meeting was an invitation to contribute to a volume on* Cognition and Psychotherapy *being edited by Michael Mahoney and Arthur Freeman. This provided an opportunity to expand the original brief paper and led to the version that follows.*

The evidence that adverse experiences with parents during childhood, such as those described in the previous lecture, play a large part in causing cognitive disturbance is now substantial. For example, at least some cases in which perceptions and attributions are distorted and some states of amnesia, both minor and major, including cases of multiple personality, can be shown with considerable confidence to be the outcome of such experiences. Yet systematic research into these causal sequences is still scarce, and it is clearly a field calling urgently for a major research effort. Why then has it been so woefully neglected?

One adverse influence, referred to in the preceding lecture, is the strong tradition within the psychoanalytic school of thought of focusing attention on fantasy and away from the real-life experiences a person may have had during childhood. Another is the undoubted difficulty of doing systematic research in the field. For example, those engaged in seeing only adult patients are usually ill-placed to investigate events alleged to have occurred many years earlier. Those whose childhoods have been spent amongst reasonably stable families and who, like all too many psychiatrists and psychotherapists, are ignorant of the recent family and child development literature have no norms against which to match their patients' stories. Above all clinicians are often faced with a blanket of silence, from patient and family alike, which neither their training nor their experience has qualified them to penetrate. It is little wonder therefore that the likelihood that many cases of psychiatric disorder, both mild and grave, have had their origins in adverse events of childhood has been discounted or else completely ignored – not only by general psychiatrists but by psychotherapists as well. Even the fact that some children are physically or sexually assaulted by their own parents, often repeatedly and over long periods, has been missing from discussions of causal factors in psychiatry.

At long last the scene is changing. First, knowledge of parent–child interactions in general, including a wide range of potentially pathogenic relationships and events, is increasing in both quality and quantity as systematic research is applied. Secondly the psychological consequences for the children exposed to these relationships and events are becoming much better understood and documented. As a result there are now many occasions when a clinician is on reasonably firm ground in drawing aetiological conclusions. This is so especially when (a) his patient presents problems and symptoms which resemble the known consequences of certain types of experience and (b) when in the course of skilled history-taking, or perhaps much later during therapy, he is told of experiences of these same types. In reaching his conclusion the reasoning a psychiatrist uses differs in no way from that of a physician who, having diagnosed a patient as suffering from mitral stenosis, proceeds unhesitatingly to attribute the condition to an attack of rheumatic fever suffered by the patient many years earlier.

When considering childhood antecedents of cognitive disorders a good place to start is with amnesia.

In one of his classical papers on analytic technique Freud (1914) made an important generalization the truth of which probably every psychotherapist would endorse:

> Forgetting impressions, scenes or experiences nearly always reduces itself to shutting them off. When the patient talks about these 'forgotten' things he seldom fails to add: 'As a matter of fact I've always known it; only I've never thought of it.'(1914, 148)

Such observations call for explanations of at least three kinds. First, are there special features that characterize the impressions, scenes, and experiences that tend to become shut off? Secondly, how do we best conceive of the processes by which memories become shut off and apparently forgotten? Thirdly, what are the causal conditions, internal and external to the personality, that activate the shutting-off process?

The scenes and experiences that tend to become shut off, though often continuing to be extremely influential in affecting thought, feeling, and behaviour, fall into at least three distinct categories: (a) those that parents wish their children not to know about; (b) those in which parents have treated children in ways the children find too unbearable to think about; (c) those in which children have done, or perhaps thought, things about which they feel unbearably guilty or ashamed.

Since a great deal of attention has for long been given to the third category, here I discuss only the first two. We start with the first.

Children not infrequently observe scenes that parents would prefer they did not observe; they form impressions that parents would prefer they did not form; and they have experiences that parents would like to believe they have not had. Evidence shows that many of these children, aware of how their parents feel, proceed then to conform to their parents' wishes by excluding from further processing such information as they already have; and that, having done so, they cease consciously to be aware that they have ever observed such scenes, formed such impressions, or had such experiences. Here, I believe, is a source of cognitive disturbance as common as it is neglected.

Yet evidence that parents sometimes press their children to shut off from further, conscious processing information the children already have about events that the parents wish they had never observed comes from several sources. Perhaps the most vivid concerns the efforts made by a surviving parent to obliterate his or her child's knowledge of the (other) parent's suicide.

Cain and Fast (1972) report findings from their study of a series of fourteen children, aged between 4 and 14, all of whom had lost a parent by suicide and all of whom had become psychiatrically disturbed, many of them severely so. In reviewing their data the authors were struck by the very large roles played in the children's symptomatology by their having been exposed to pathogenic situations of two types, namely situations in which intense guilt is likely to be engendered (not discussed here) and situations in which communications between parent and child are gravely distorted.

About one quarter of the children studied had personally witnessed some aspect of the parent's death and had subsequently been subjected to pressure from the surviving parent to believe that they were mistaken in what they had seen or heard, and that the death had not been due to suicide but to some illness or accident. 'A boy who watched his father kill himself with a shotgun ... was told later that night by his mother that his father died of a heart attack; a girl who discovered her father's body hanging in a closet was told he had died in a car accident; and two brothers who had found their mother with her wrists slit were told she had drowned while swimming' (Cain and Fast 1972, 102). When a child described what he had seen, the surviving parent had sought to discredit it either by ridicule or by insisting that he was confused by what he had seen on television or by some bad dream he had had. Such confusion was sometimes compounded, moreover, by the child hearing several different stories about the death from different people or even from his surviving parent.

Many of the children's psychological problems seemed directly traceable to their having been exposed to situations of these kinds. Their problems included chronic distrust of other people, inhibition of their curiosity, distrust of their own senses, and a tendency to find everything unreal.

Rosen (1955) describes an adult patient, a man of 27, who developed acute symptoms after his fiancée had jilted him, because she had found him too moody and unpredictable. The patient began to feel that the world about him and also his own being were fragmenting, and that everything was unreal. He became depressed and suicidal; and he experienced a variety of peculiar bodily sensations, which included a feeling that he was choking. His thoughts, he said, felt like cotton-wool. Sometime during the second year of therapy the analyst, struck by a series of associations the patient gave, and bearing in mind the life history, ventured a reconstruction, namely that the patient's mother may have made a suicidal attempt during the patient's childhood that he (the patient) had witnessed. No sooner had this suggestion been offered than the patient became racked with convulsive sobbing. The session proved a turning point. Subsequently the patient described how it had seemed to him that, when the analyst made his suggestion, it was not so much that he was restoring a memory as giving him (the patient) permission to talk about something he had always in some way known about.

The authenticity of the memory was vouched for by the patient's father who admitted, when pressed, that the patient's mother had made several suicide attempts during the patient's childhood. The one the patient had witnessed occurred some time during his third year. His nurse had heard sounds in the bathroom and had arrived in time to prevent his mother from strangling herself. It was not clear just how much the little boy had seen. But whenever later he had mentioned the event both father and nurse had disconfirmed his memories by alleging that it was something he must have imagined or had simply been a bad dream. The father now claimed that he had felt it would have been harmful to his son to have remembered such an incident; but he also admitted that his attitude was dictated partly by his wish that the incident be kept secret from friends and neighbours. A year or so later the nurse had been discharged because the mother had found her presence too painful a reminder of the incident.

During one of the sessions before the vital reconstruction was offered the patient had recalled the discharge of his beloved nurse as an event which he had always felt had been in some way his fault. Among many associations to it were recurrent references to his having been, as a child, witness to something that had changed his life, though he did not know what. He also had the notion that his nurse had been the one witness on his behalf. Thus, although the memory had been shut away from conscious processing, it continued to influence both what he thought and how he felt.

Elsewhere (Bowlby 1973) I have drawn attention to the far from negligible incidence of suicidal attempts made by parents, and perhaps the even higher incidence of their threatening suicide, and have remarked how little attention has been given to either attempts or threats in the psychiatric and psychotherapeutic literature. Perhaps there are many more cases similar to Rosen's than has yet been realized.

Among the many other situations that parents may wish a child had not observed, and that they may press him to suppose he never did, are those concerning their sexual activities. An example of this was told to me by a speech therapist who was trying to help an extremely disturbed little girl who hardly spoke at all. That she was well able to speak was, however, shown on certain dramatic occasions. She would sit a teddy-bear on a chair in a corner, then go over and, shaking her finger at him, would scold him in tones of extreme severity: 'You're *naughty – naughty Teddy –* you *didn't* see that – you *didn't* see that, I tell you!' This she repeated again and again with increasing vehemence. What the scenes were that Teddy was being instructed he never saw was not difficult to guess: the little girl's mother was a teenage prostitute.

Clearly the purpose of these pressures by parents is to ensure that their children develop and maintain a wholly favourable picture of them. In the examples thus far given the form of pressure exerted is crude. More frequent perhaps and just as damaging are instances in which the pressures are more subtle.

During the past two decades renewed attention has been paid to incest, both to its unrecognized high incidence and to its pathogenic effects on children. Much the commonest forms are between father and daughter or step-father and step-daughter. Among the various problems and symptoms in the children and adolescents concerned that are believed to be due to these experiences, the commonest include withdrawal from all intimate relationships, sleep disturbances, and suicidal intentions (Meiselman 1978; Adams-Tucker 1982). An account of conditions likely to cause cognitive disturbance was given me by a colleague, Brendan MacCarthy, but never published. He suspected that disturbance is especially likely when the children are prepubertal. In what follows I draw on his conclusions.

When a sexual liaison develops between a father and his adolescent daughter, MacCarthy reports, the liaison is usually acknowledged by the father during the course of daily life by such means as secret glances, secret touching, and innuendoes. In the case of a younger child, however, a father is likely to make no such acknowledgements. Instead he behaves during the day as though the nightly episodes never occurred; and this total failure to acknowledge them is commonly maintained even long after the daughter has reached adolescence.

MacCarthy describes the case of a married woman, Mrs A, whom he treated for depression, reliance on tranquillizers, and alcohol. She mentioned the ten years of sexual interference she had suffered from her adoptive father only after she had been in therapy for four months. It had begun when she was 5 or 6, soon after her adoptive mother had died, and had continued until she was 16, when she had fled. Among her many problems were frigidity and finding intercourse disgusting, and a sense of inner blackness, of 'a black stain'. Her problems had become exacerbated when her own daughter was 4 years old. Whenever the daughter became affectionate to her father and sat near him, Mrs A felt agitated, protective, and jealous; on these occasions she could never leave them alone together. During therapy she was obsequious and terrified, and intensely vigilant of the analyst's every move.

In regard to the incestuous relationship, Mrs A described how her adoptive father would never at any time during the day

105

allude to his nocturnal visits to her room, which had always remained darkened. On the contrary, he had lectured her incessantly on the dangers of allowing boys to go too far, and on the importance of chastity before marriage. When at the age of 16 she had fled the home, he not only insisted she tell no one, but added sarcastically: 'And if you do no one will believe you.' This could well have been so since her adoptive father was a headmaster and the local mayor.

In commenting on this and similar cases MacCarthy emphasizes the cognitive split between the respected and perhaps loved father of daytime and the very different father of the strange events of the night before. Warned on no account to breathe a word to anyone, including her mother, the child looks to her father for some confirmation of those events and is naturally bewildered when there is no response. Did it really happen or did I dream it? Have I two fathers? Small wonder if, in later years, all men are distrusted, and the professional stance of a male therapist is seen as a mere façade that hides a predatory intent. Small wonder also that the injunction on no account to tell anyone remains operative, and that the expectation that in any case no one would believe you ensures silence. How often, we may wonder, do ill-informed therapists discourage a patient from telling the truth and, should she do so nonetheless, confirm her expectation that no one will believe her story?

In the examples so far described the information a parent is pressing a child to shut away is information relating to events in the outside world. In other situations the information to be shut away relates to events in the child's private world of feeling. Nowhere does this occur more commonly than in situations of separation and loss.

When a parent dies the surviving parent or other relative may not only provide the children with inadequate or misleading information but he or she may also indicate that it would not be appropriate for the child even to be distressed. This may be explicit: A. Miller (1979) describes how, when a 6–year–old's mother died, his aunt told him: 'You must be brave; don't cry; now go to your room and play nicely.' At other times the indication is only implicit. Not infrequently widows or widowers, afraid to express their own distress, in effect encourage their children to shut away all the feeling they are having about their loss. Palgi (1973) describes how a small boy whose mother was chiding him for not shedding tears over his father's death retorted: 'How can I cry when I have never seen your tears?'

There are in fact many situations in which a child is expressly told not to cry. For example, a child of 5 whose nanny is leaving is told not to cry because that would make it more difficult for nanny. A child whose parents leave him in hospital or residential nursery insist he should not cry, otherwise they will not visit him. A child whose parents are frequently away and who leave him with one of a succession of au pair girls is not encouraged to recognize how lonely, and perhaps angry, he feels at their constant absence. When parents separate, it is often made plain to a child that he is not expected to miss the departing parent or to pine for the parent's return. Not only is sorrow and crying condemned as inappropriate in such situations but older children and adults may jeer at a distressed child for being a cry-baby. Is there any wonder that in such circumstances feeling should become shut away?

All these situations are plain enough but have, I believe, been seriously neglected as causes of information and feeling becoming excluded from consciousness. There are, however, other situations also, more subtle and hidden but no less common, that have the same effect. One such is when a mother, who herself had a childhood deprived of love, seeks from her own child the love she has hitherto lacked. In doing this she is inverting the normal parent–child relationship, requiring the child to act as parent whilst she becomes a child. To someone unaware of what is going on it may appear that the child is being 'overindulged', but a closer look shows that mother is placing a heavy burden on him. What is of special relevance here is that more often than not the child is expected to be grateful for such care as he receives and not to notice the demands being made upon him. One result of this is that, in conformity with his mother's wishes, he builds up a one-sided picture of her as wholly loving and generous, thereby shutting away from conscious processing much information also reaching him that she is often selfish, demanding, and ungrateful. Another result is that, also in conformity with his mother's wishes, he admits to consciousness only feelings of love and gratitude towards her and shuts away every feeling of anger he may have against her for expecting him to care for her and preventing him from making his own friends and living his own life.

A related situation is one in which a parent, having had a traumatic childhood, is apprehensive of being reminded of past miseries and so becoming depressed. As a result her children are required always to appear happy and to avoid any expression of sorrow, loneliness, or anger. As one patient put it to me after a good deal of therapy: 'I see now that I was terribly lonely as a child but I was never allowed to know it.'

Most children are indulgent towards their parents, preferring to see them in a favourable light and eager to overlook many deficiencies. Yet they do not willingly conform to seeing a parent only in the light the parent requires or to feeling towards him or her only in the way demanded. To ensure that, pressure must be exerted. Pressure can take different forms but all forms depend for their effectiveness on the child's insistent desire to be loved and protected. Alice Miller (1979), who has given these problems much attention, reports the words of an adult patient who was born the eldest child of an insecure professional woman:

> I was the jewel in my mother's crown. She often said: 'Maja can be relied upon, she will cope.' And I did cope. I brought up the smaller children for her so that she could get on with her professional career. She became more and more famous, but I never saw her happy. How often I longed for her in the evenings. The little ones cried and I comforted them but I myself never cried. Who would have wanted a crying child? I could only win my mother's love if I was competent, understanding and controlled, if I never questioned her actions nor showed her how much I missed her; that would have limited her freedom which she needed so much. That would have turned her against me.

In other families pressures are less subtle. One form, threatening to abandon a child as a means of controlling him, is an extremely powerful weapon, especially with a young child. Faced with such threats, how could a child do other than conform to his parents' wishes by excluding from further processing all that he knows they wish him to forget? Elsewhere I have given reasons for believing that threats of this sort are responsible for much acute and chronic anxiety (Bowlby 1973) and also for a person responding to bereavement in later life with chronic depression in which the dominant belief is one of having been deliberately abandoned, as a punishment, by the dead person (Bowlby 1980).

The hypothesis advanced, that various forms of cognitive disturbance seen in children and also in later life are to be traced to influences acting initially during the pre-adolescent years, is compatible with indications that during these years children's minds are especially sensitive to outside influence. Evidence of this, already emphasized, is the extent to which young children are vulnerable to threats by parents to reject or even abandon them. After a child has reached adolescence, clearly his vulnerability to such threats diminishes.

The extent to which the minds of pre-adolescent children are prone to the influence of parents is well illustrated by an experiment of Gill (1970). The sample comprised 10-year-old children, drawn from a London primary school, and their parents. Of the forty non-immigrant families invited to participate, twenty-five agreed. Each family was visited in its own home and a series of ten pictures shown on a screen, each for two minutes.

Of the pictures used, five came from picture book or film and the rest from thematic apperception tests. Some were emotionally benign, for example, a mother watching a small girl holding a baby. Some showed scenes of an aggressive and/or frightening sort. Three depicted a sexual theme: a woman obviously pregnant lying on a bed; a couple embracing on the grass; and a woman clutching the shoulders of a man who seems to be pulling away, with the picture of a semi-nude woman in the background.

The series of ten pictures was presented three times in succession. On the first showing, father, mother, and child were asked to write down independently what they saw happening in the picture. On the second members of the family were asked to discuss each picture for the two minutes it was shown.

During the third showing, each member was asked again to write down independently what they now saw happening.

When the children's responses to the three pictures depicting sexual themes were examined, it was found that, whereas half the children (12) described the sexual themes in a fairly direct matter-of-fact way, the other half failed to do so. For example, to the picture of the obviously pregnant woman, one child's candid response ran: 'She's having a rest. I can see that she's expecting a baby. She's asleep, I think.' Descriptions of the same picture by other children omitted all reference to pregnancy. 'Somebody is asleep in bed,' and 'There's a man on a bed. He is asleep.'

A second step was to analyse how the parents discussed the picture in the child's presence during the second showing. This was done by a psychologist blind to the children's responses. Here again it was evident that, whereas some parents were candid about the scene depicted, others made no reference to it and/or expressed disgust. For example, in the case of the pregnant woman, the mother of one child remarked frankly and on three occasions that the woman was expecting a baby and was having an afternoon rest. By contrast, the parents of another child completed their two-minute discussion without any such reference. Instead they concentrated on emotionally neutral details such as the woman's hairstyle, the material of her dressing gown, and the quality of the furniture. Not surprisingly there was a high correlation between the way the children responded to the pictures and the way the parents had discussed them subsequently.

On the third showing the descriptions given by all the children improved in accuracy; but those of the twelve who had responded candidly on the first showing improved more than did the descriptions given by the thirteen who had failed to report the pictures' content on the first occasion.

There could be little doubt that during their discussion of the pictures some of the parents were, consciously or unconsciously, avoiding reference to the content of the pictures. It was a reasonable inference also that their children's failure to describe the sexual theme on the first showing was in some way influenced by the 'climate' they had experienced in their homes. What the experiment could not show, of course, was whether these children had truly failed to perceive the scene depicted or whether they had perceived it but had failed to report what they saw. Since pre-adolescent children tend to be slow and often uncertain in their perceptions, my guess would be that at least some of the children in the experiment had truly failed to register the nature of what was happening. Others may have known intuitively that the scene was one they were not supposed to know about and so avoided seeing it.

At first sight the notion that information of a certain meaning can be shut off, or selectively excluded from perception, appears paradoxical. How, it is asked, can a person selectively exclude from processing a particular stimulus unless he first perceives the stimulus which he wishes to exclude? This stumbling block disappears, however, once perception is conceived as a multi-stage process as nowadays it is. Indeed experimental work on human information processing undertaken during the past decade or so enables us to have a much better idea of the nature of the shutting-off processes we have been discussing than was possible when Freud and others in the psychodynamic tradition were first formulating the theories of defence that have been so very influential ever since. In what follows I give a brief sketch of this new approach.

Studies of human perception (Erdelyi 1974; Norman 1976) have shown that, before a person is aware of seeing something or hearing something, the sensory inflow coming through his eyes or ears, has already passed through many stages of selection, interpretation, and appraisal, during the course of which a large proportion of the original inflow has been excluded. The reason for this extensive exclusion is that the channels responsible for the most advanced processing are of limited capacity and must therefore be protected from overload. To ensure that what is most relevant gets through and that only the less relevant is excluded, selection of inflow is under central, or we might say ego, control. Although this processing is done at extraordinary speeds and almost all of it outside awareness, much of the inflow has nonetheless been carried to a very advanced stage of processing before being excluded. The results of experiments on dichotic listening provide striking examples.

111

In this type of experiment two different messages are transmitted simultaneously to a person, one message to each ear. The person is then told to attend to one of these messages only, say the one being received by the right ear. To ensure he gives it continuous attention, he is required to 'shadow' that message by repeating it word for word as he is hearing it. Keeping the two messages distinct is found to be fairly easy, and at the end of the session the subject is usually totally unaware of the content of the unattended message. Yet there are significant exceptions. For example, should his own name or some personally significant word occur in the unattended message, he may well notice and remember it. This shows that, even though consciously unattended, this message is being subjected to continuous and fairly advanced processing during which its meaning is being monitored and its content appraised as more or less relevant; and all this without the person being in any way aware of what was going on.

In the ordinary course of a person's life the criteria applied to sensory inflow that determine what information is to be accepted and what is to be excluded are readily intelligible as reflecting what is at any one time in the person's best interests. Thus, when he is hungry, sensory inflow concerned with food is given priority, whilst much else that might at other times be of interest to him is excluded. Yet, should danger threaten, priorities would quickly change so that inflow concerned with issues of danger and safety would take precedence and inflow concerned with food be temporarily excluded. This change in the criteria governing what inflow is to be accepted and what excluded is effected by evaluating systems central to the personality.

In thus summarizing the findings from a neighbouring discipline the main points I wish to emphasize are first that throughout a person's life he is engaged in excluding, or shutting out, a large proportion of all the information that is reaching him; secondly that he does so only after its relevance to himself has been assessed; and thirdly that this process of selective exclusion is usually carried out without his being in any way aware of its happening.

Admittedly, so far, most of these experiments have been concerned with the processing of current sensory inflow, namely with perception, and not with the utilization of information already stored in memory, namely with recall. Yet it seems likely that the same general principles apply. In each case criteria are set by one or more central evaluating systems and it is these criteria that govern what information is passed through for further, and conscious, processing and what is excluded. Thus, thanks to the work of cognitive psychologists, there is no longer any difficulty in imagining, and describing in operational terms, a mental apparatus capable of shutting off information of certain specified types and of doing so without the person being aware of what is happening.

Let us consider next the second category of scenes and experiences that tend to become shut off and forgotten, whilst at the same time continuing to be more or less influential in affecting a person's thoughts, feeling, and behaviour. These are the scenes and experiences in which parents have treated children in ways the children find too unbearable to think about or remember. Here again not only is there amnesia, partial or complete, for the sequence of events but also exclusion from consciousness of the thoughts, feelings, and impulses to action that are the natural responses to such events. This results in major disorders of personality which in their commoner and less severe forms tend to be diagnosed as cases of narcissism or false self and in their more severe forms may be labelled as a fugue, a psychosis, or a case of multiple personality. The experiences which give rise to such disorders have probably continued or been repeated over several years of childhood, perhaps starting during the first two or three but usually continuing during the fourth, fifth, sixth, and seventh years, and no doubt often for longer still. The experiences themselves include repeated rejection by parents combined with contempt for a child's desire for love, care, and comforting, and, especially in the more severe forms, physical violence (battering), repeated and sometimes systematic, and sexual exploitation by father or mother's boy-friend. Not infrequently a child in this predicament is subjected to a combination of such experiences.

We start at the less severe end of what appears to be a spectrum of related syndromes.

An example of a patient labelled as 'false self' has already been given in an earlier lecture (see p. 53). This concerned a severely depressed and suicidal young graduate who recalled during analysis how his mother had consistently rejected him, ignored his crying, locked herself away in her room for days on end, and had several times left home. Fortunately he had been in the hands of a therapist who understood his problem, gave full credence to the childhood experiences he described, and sympathetic recognition both of his unrequited yearning for love and care and also for the violent feelings towards his mother that her treatment of him had aroused, and which initially were directed towards herself (the therapist). A patient with rather similar problems but whose experiences included also a period of eighteen months in an impersonal institution, starting when she was 4 years old, is reported in lecture 4. Although both these patients made rewarding progress during treatment, both remained more sensitive than others to further misfortune.

A number of patients, both children and adults, whose disorders appear to have originated in similar though mainly worse experiences and to have resulted in personality splitting of an even greater degree have been described by therapists during the past decade. An example is Geraldine, aged 11, who had been found wandering in a dazed state and who had lost all memory both of her mother's terminal illness and of events of the three subsequent years. At the end of a long period of therapy, described in great detail by McCann (in Furman 1974), Geraldine summed up the experiences which had preceded her amnesia: 'With Mama, I was scared to death to step out of line. I saw with my own eyes how she attacked, in words and actions, my Dad and sister and, after all, I was just a little kid, very powerless. ... How could I ever be mad at Mama – she was really the only security I had ... I blotted out all feelings – things happened that were more than I could endure – I had to keep going. If I had really let things hit me, I wouldn't be here. I'd be dead or in a mental hospital.'*

The complex psychological state of Geraldine and also the childhood experiences held to have been responsible for it bear

---

* A long abstract of McCann's account is given in *Loss* (Bowlby 1980, 338–44).

close resemblance to the state of patients suffering from multiple personality and to the childhood experiences held responsible for them.

In an article by Bliss (1980), based on clinical examinations and therapy carried out by means of hypnosis, a description is given of fourteen patients, all female, diagnosed as suffering from multiple personality. The hypothesis Bliss advances is that the subordinate personalities that take possession of a patient from time to time are the cognitive creations of the principal personality when, as a child of between 4 and 7 years, she was subjected for extended periods to intensely distressing events. According to Bliss, each such personality is created initially to serve a distinct purpose or role. Judged from the examples he gives, the roles are of three main kinds. The simplest and most benign is to act as a companion and protector when the creating personality is feeling lonely or isolated, as, for example, when parents are persistently hostile and/or absent and there is no one else to turn to. A second role is to be anaesthetic to unbearably distressing events, as in the case of a child of 4 or 5 who shared a room with her mother who, dying of cancer, spent hours screaming in pain. The third role is more complex, namely to shoulder the responsibility for thinking, feeling, and acting in ways that the patient cannot bear to accept as her own. Examples given by Bliss include feeling violent hatred of a mother who had attempted to kill the patient when a child, a hatred amounting to an intent actually to murder her; feeling and acting sexually after having been raped as a child; and feeling frightened and tearful after crying had led to punishments and threats from parents.

Since findings derived from hypnotic procedures are controversial, it is important to note that a clinical research group at the University of California at Irvine, which uses conventional procedures and which has studied a number of cases (Reagor, personal communication), has reached conclusions very similar to those of Bliss.* The therapeutic procedures proposed have

---

* See also Bliss (1986). Further evidence that multiple personality disorder develops during childhood as a defence against overwhelming trauma, usually severe abuse, is reported in Kluft (1985).

much in common also and are, moreover, strongly in keeping with the concepts of therapy described in the final lecture.

Lastly, a number of child psychiatrists and child psycho-therapists (e.g. Stroh 1974; Rosenfeld 1975; Bloch 1978; Hopkins 1984), have described children whose thought and behaviour make them appear either nearly or frankly psychotic, who show pronouncedly paranoid ideas, and whose condition, the evidence suggests, can be attributed to persistently abusive treatment by parents. Such children are often charming and endearing one moment and savagely hostile the next, the change occurring suddenly and for no apparent reason. Their greatest violence, moreover, is most likely to be directed against the very indi-vidual to whom they appear, indeed are, most closely attached. Not infrequently these children are tormented by intense fear that some monster will attack them and they spend their time trying to escape the expected attack. In at least some of these cases there is cogent evidence that what is feared is an attack by one or other parent but, that expectation being unbearably frightening, the expected attack is attributed to an imaginary monster.

As an example, let us consider the case of 6-year-old Sylvia, reported by Hopkins (1984), one of whose principal symptoms was a terror that the chairs and other items of furniture, which she called Daleks, would fly across the room to strike her. 'Her terror was intense and when she kept cowering and ducking as though about to receive a blow from a Dalek or some other monster, I thought she was hallucinating.' From the first Sylvia also expressed the fear that her therapist would hit her like her mother did. Not only did she constantly attack her therapist but she often threatened to kill her.

The father had died in an automobile accident two years earlier. During many months of twice weekly interviews with a social worker, the mother was extremely guarded and told little of family relations. At length, however, after nearly two years the veil was lifted. She admitted her own massive rejection of Sylvia from the time of her birth, and the murderous feelings both she and father had had for her. Her treatment of Sylvia, she confessed, had been 'utterly brutal'. The father had had an extremely violent temper and in his not infrequent rages had broken the furniture and thrown it across the room. He had frequently beaten Sylvia and had even thrown her across the room.

Thus the identity of the Daleks was not in doubt. Behind the 'fantasy' of a Dalek attack lay a serious reality-based expectation of an attack by father or mother. As Bloch (1978) has put it, a basic premise of the therapeutic approach she and others like her advocate for these cases is that what is so facilely dubbed as fantasy be recognized as a reflection of a grim reality, and that an early therapeutic task is to identify the real-life experiences lying close behind the deceptive camouflage.

Not only are the childhood experiences of these near-psychotic children the same as those believed characteristic of adult patients with multiple personality, but the states of mind described by the respective therapists have features strikingly similar too. It seems highly likely therefore that the two conditions are closely related. It should be noted furthermore that these findings give support to the hypothesis advanced by Niederland (1959a and b, discussed by Bowlby 1973) that the paranoid delusions of Judge Schreber, on which Freud based his theory of paranoia, were distorted versions of the extraordinary pedagogic regime to which the patient's father had subjected him from the early months of life.

In this contribution, as in almost all my work, I have focused attention on psychopathology and some of the conditions that give rise to it. My reason for doing so is the belief that only with a better understanding of aetiology and psychopathology will it be possible to develop therapeutic techniques and, more especially, preventive measures that will be at once effective and economical in skilled manpower.

My therapeutic approach is far from original. The basic hypothesis can be stated simply. So long as current modes of perceiving and construing situations, and the feelings and actions that ensue therefrom, are determined by emotionally significant events and experiences that have become shut away from further conscious processing, the personality will be prone to cognition, affect, and behaviour maladapted to the current situation. When yearning for love and care is shut away, it will continue to be inaccessible. When there is anger, it will continue to be directed at inappropriate targets. Similarly anxiety will continue to be aroused by inappropriate situations and hostile behaviour be expected from inappropriate sources. The therapeutic task is therefore to help the patient discover what these events and experiences may have been so that the thoughts, feelings, and behaviour that the situations arouse, and that continue to be so troublesome, can be linked again to the situations that aroused them. Then the true targets of his yearning and anger and the true sources of his anxiety and fear will become plain. Not only will such discoveries show that his modes of cognition, feeling, and behaviour are far more intelligible, given the circumstances in which they originated, than they had seemed before but, once the patient has grasped how and why he is responding as he is, he will be in a position to reappraise his responses and, should he wish, to undertake their radical restructuring. Since such reappraisal and restructuring can be achieved only by the patient himself, the emphasis in this formulation of the therapist's task is on helping the patient first to discover *for himself* what the relevant scenes and experiences probably were and secondly to spend time pondering on how they have continued to influence him. Only then will he be in a position to undertake the reorganization of his modes of construing the world, thinking about it, and acting in it which are called for.

The concepts of therapeutic process outlined here are similar to those described in much greater detail by others. Examples are publications by Peterfreund (1983) and by Guidano and Liotti (1983). Although the authors of these two books started their therapeutic work from radically different positions, namely traditional versions of psychoanalysis and of behaviour therapy respectively, the principles that now guide their work show a striking convergence. Similarly current forms of bereavement therapy, which focus on distressing events in the comparatively recent past, are found to be based on the very same principles, even when developed within equally different traditions (Raphael 1977; Melges and DeMaso 1980). However divergent tactics may still appear, strategic thinking is on a convergent course.

LECTURE 7

The role of
attachment in
personality development

*Evidence regarding the role of attachment in personality development
has been accumulating apace during the nineteen-eighties. Earlier findings have been replicated on samples of diverse origin; methods of
observation have been refined and new methods introduced; and the role
of easy two-way communication between parent and child in making for
healthy emotional development has been emphasized. Since I believe this
new work to have far-reaching clinical implications, my aim in this
lecture has been to present a review of these findings in a form suited to
those working as psychotherapists in the mental health field.*

*For the convenience of the reader I begin by restating in summary
form some of the features most distinctive of attachment theory.*

Some distinctive features of attachment theory

It will be remembered that attachment theory was formulated to
explain certain patterns of behaviour, characteristic not only of
infants and young children but also adolescents and adults, that
were formerly conceptualized in terms of dependency and over-
dependency. In its original formulation observations of how
young children respond when placed in a strange place with
strange people, and the effects such experiences have on a
child's subsequent relations with his parents, were especially
influential. In all subsequent work theory has continued to be

119

tied closely to detailed observations and interview data of how individuals respond in particular situations. Historically the theory was developed out of the object-relations tradition in psychoanalysis; but it has drawn also on concepts from evolution theory, ethology, control theory, and cognitive psychology. One result is the reformulation of psychoanalytic metapsychology in ways compatible with modern biology and psychology and in conformity with the commonly accepted criteria of natural science (see Lecture 4).

Attachment theory emphasizes:

(a) the primary status and biological function of intimate emotional bonds between individuals, the making and maintaining of which are postulated to be controlled by a cybernetic system situated within the central nervous system, utilizing working models of self and attachment figure in relationship with each other.*

(b) the powerful influence on a child's development of the ways he is treated by his parents, especially his mother-figure, and

(c) that present knowledge of infant and child development requires that a theory of developmental pathways should replace theories that invoke specific phases of development in which it is held a person may become fixated and/or to which he may regress.

The primacy of intimate emotional bonds

Attachment theory regards the propensity to make intimate emotional bonds to particular individuals as a basic component

---

* In earlier publications I have sometimes used the term 'representational model' as a synonym for 'working model' because representation has been the more familiar concept in clinical literature. In a dynamic psychology, however, working model is the more appropriate term, and it is also the term that is now coming into use among cognitive psychologists (e.g. Johnson-Laird 1983). Within the attachment framework the concept of working model of an attachment figure is in many respects equivalent to, and replaces, the traditional psychoanalytic concept of internal object.

of human nature, already present in germinal form in the neonate and continuing through adult life into old age. During infancy and childhood bonds are with parents (or parent substitutes) who are looked to for protection, comfort, and support. During healthy adolescence and adult life these bonds persist, but are complemented by new bonds, commonly of a heterosexual nature. Although food and sex sometimes play important roles in attachment relationships, the relationship exists in its own right and has a key survival function of its own, namely protection. Initially the only means of communication between infant and mother is through emotional expression and its accompanying behaviour. Although supplemented later by speech, emotionally mediated communication nonetheless persists as a principal feature of intimate relationships throughout life.

Within the attachment framework therefore intimate emotional bonds are seen as neither subordinate to nor derivative from food and sex. Nor is the urgent desire for comfort and support in adversity regarded as childish, as dependency theory implies. Instead the capacity to make intimate emotional bonds with other individuals, sometimes in the careseeking role and sometimes in the caregiving one, is regarded as a principal feature of effective personality functioning and mental health.

As a rule careseeking is shown by a weaker and less experienced individual towards someone regarded as stronger and/or wiser. A child, or older person in the careseeking role, keeps within range of the caregiver, the degree of closeness or of ready accessibility depending on circumstances: hence the concept of attachment behaviour.

Caregiving, the major role of parents and complementary to attachment behaviour, is regarded in the same light as careseeking, namely as a basic component of human nature (see Lecture 1).

Exploring the environment, including play and varied activities with peers, is seen as a third basic component and one antithetic to attachment behaviour. When an individual (of any age) is feeling secure he is likely to explore away from his attachment figure. When alarmed, anxious, tired, or unwell he feels an urge towards proximity. Thus we see the typical pattern of inter-

121

action between child and parent known as exploration from a secure base, first described by Ainsworth (1967). Provided the parent is known to be accessible and will be responsive when called upon, a healthy child feels secure enough to explore. At first these explorations are limited both in time and space. Around the middle of the third year, however, a secure child begins to become confident enough to increase time and distance away – first to half-days and later to whole days. As he grows into adolescence, his excursions are extended to weeks or months, but a secure home base remains indispensable nonetheless for optimal functioning and mental health. Note that the concept of secure base is a central feature of the theory of psychotherapy proposed.

During the early months of life an infant shows many of the component responses of what will later become attachment behaviour, but the organized pattern does not develop until the second half of the first year. From birth onwards he shows a germinal capacity to engage in social interaction and pleasure in doing so (Stern 1985): thus there is no autistic or narcissistic phase. Within days, moreover, he is able to distinguish between his mother-figure and others by means of her smell and by hearing her voice, and also by the way she holds him. Visual discrimination is not reliable until the second quarter. Initially crying is the only means available to him for signalling his need for care, and contentment the only means for signalling that he has been satisfied. During the second month, however, his social smile acts strongly to encourage his mother in her ministrations and his repertoire of emotional communications rapidly extends (Izard 1982; Emde 1983).

The development of attachment behaviour as an organized system, having as its goal the keeping of proximity or of accessibility to a discriminated mother-figure, requires that the child should have developed the cognitive capacity to keep his mother in mind when she is not present: this capacity develops during the second six months of life. Thus from nine months onwards the great majority of infants respond to being left with a strange person by protest and crying, and also by more or less prolonged fretting and rejection of the stranger. These observations demonstrate that during these months an infant is becoming capable of representation and that his working model of his mother is becoming available to him for purposes of comparison during her absence and for recognition after her return. Complementary to his model of his mother, he develops a working model of himself in interaction with her; likewise for father.

A major feature of attachment theory is the hypothesis that attachment behaviour is organized by means of a control system within the central nervous system, analogous to the physiological control systems that maintain physiological measures such as blood pressure and body temperature within set limits. Thus the theory proposes that, in a way analogous to physiological homeostasis, the attachment control system maintains a person's relation to his attachment figure between certain limits of distance and accessibility, using increasingly sophisticated methods of communication for doing so. As such, the effects of its operation can be regarded as an example of what can usefully be termed environmental homeostasis (Bowlby 1969, 1982). By postulating a control system of this sort (with analogous systems controlling other forms of behaviour) attachment theory contains within itself a theory of motivation that can replace traditional theories which invoke a postulated build-up of energy or drive. Among several advantages of control theory are that it gives as much attention to the conditions terminating a behavioural sequence as to those initiating it and is proving a fruitful framework for empirical research.

The presence of an attachment control system and its linkage to the working models of self and attachment figure(s) that are built in the mind during childhood are held to be central features of personality functioning throughout life.

Patterns of attachment and conditions determining their development

The second area to which attachment theory pays special attention is the role of a child's parents in determining how he develops. There is today impressive and mounting evidence that the pattern of attachment that an individual develops during the years of immaturity – infancy, childhood, and adolescence – is profoundly influenced by the way his parents (or other parent figures) treat him. This evidence derives from a number of systematic research studies, the most impressive being prospective studies of socio-emotional development during the first five years undertaken by developmental psychologists who are also clinically sophisticated. Pioneered by Ainsworth (Ainsworth, Blehar, Waters, and Wall 1978; Ainsworth 1985) and expanded, notably by Main (Main, Kaplan, and Cassidy 1985) and Sroufe (1983, 1985) in the United States and by Grossmann (Grossmann, Grossmann, and Schwan 1986) in Germany, these studies are now multiplying fast. Their findings are remarkably consistent and have the clearest of clinical significance.

Three principal patterns of attachment, first described by Ainsworth and her colleagues in 1971, are now reliably identified, together with the family conditions that promote them. These are first the pattern of secure attachment in which the individual is confident that his parent (or parent figure) will be available, responsive, and helpful should he encounter adverse or frightening situations. With this assurance, he feels bold in his explorations of the world. This pattern is promoted by a parent, in the early years especially by mother, being readily available, sensitive to her child's signals, and lovingly responsive when he seeks protection and/or comfort.

A second pattern is that of anxious resistant attachment in which the individual is uncertain whether his parent will be available or responsive or helpful when called upon. Because of this uncertainty he is always prone to separation anxiety, tends to be clinging, and is anxious about exploring the world. This pattern, in which conflict is evident, is promoted by a parent being available and helpful on some occasions but not on others, and by separations and, as clinical findings show, by threats of abandonment used as a means of control.

A third pattern is that of anxious avoidant attachment in which the individual has no confidence that, when he seeks care, he will be responded to helpfully but, on the contrary, expects to be rebuffed. When in marked degree such an individual attempts to live his life without the love and support of others, he tries to become emotionally self-sufficient and may later be diagnosed as narcissistic or as having a false self of the type

124

described by Winnicott (1960). This pattern, in which conflict is more hidden, is the result of the individual's mother constantly rebuffing him when he approaches her for comfort or protection. The most extreme cases result from repeated rejections.

Although in most cases the pattern observed conforms fairly closely to one or another of the three well-recognized types, there have been puzzling exceptions. During the assessment procedure used in these studies (the Ainsworth Strange Situation), in which infant and mother are observed in interaction during a series of brief episodes, certain infants have appeared to be disoriented and/or disorganized. One infant appears dazed; another freezes immobile; a third engages in some stereotypy; a fourth starts a movement, then stops unaccountably. After much study Main and her colleagues have concluded that these peculiar forms of behaviour occur in infants who are exhibiting a disorganized version of one of the three typical patterns, more often than not the anxious resistant one (Main and Weston 1981; Main and Solomon in press). Some instances are seen in infants known to have been physically abused and/or grossly neglected by the parent (Crittenden 1985). Others occur in dyads in which the mother is suffering from a severe form of bipolar affective illness and who treats her child in an erratic and unpredictable way (Radke-Yarrow *et al.* 1985). Yet others are shown by the infants of mothers who are still preoccupied with mourning a parental figure lost during the mother's childhood and by those of mothers who themselves suffered physical or sexual abuse as children (Main and Hesse, in press). Cases showing these deviant patterns are clearly of great clinical concern, and much attention is now being given to them.

Knowledge of the origins of these deviant patterns confirms in the clearest possible way the influence on a child's pattern of attachment of the parent's way of treating his or her child. Yet further confirmatory evidence comes from detailed observations of the way different mothers treat their children during a laboratory session arranged when the child is $2\frac{1}{2}$ years old (Matas, Arend, and Sroufe 1978). In this study the child is given a small but difficult task for the solution of which he requires a little assistance, and his mother is free to interact with him. In this situation, it is found, the way she treats him correlates closely with the pattern of attachment her child showed towards her eighteen months earlier. Thus the mother of a child earlier assessed as securely attached is found to be attentive and sensitive to his performance and to respond to his successes and difficulties in a way that is helpful and encouraging. Conversely the mother of a child earlier assessed as insecure is found to be less attentive and/or less sensitive. In some cases her responses are ill-timed and unhelpful; in others she may take little notice of what he is doing or how he is feeling; in yet others she may actively discourage or reject his bids for help and encouragement. Note that the pattern of interaction adopted by the mother of a secure infant provides an excellent model for the pattern of therapeutic intervention advocated here.

In thus underlining the very great influence that a child's mother has on his development, it is necessary also to consider what has led a mother to adopt the style of mothering she does. One major influence on this is the amount of emotional support, or lack of it, she herself is receiving at the time. Another is the form of mothering that she herself received when a child. Once these factors are recognized, as they have been by many analytically oriented clinicians long since, the idea of blaming parents evaporates and is replaced by a therapeutic approach. Since the emotional problems of parents stemming from the past and their effects on children has now become a field for systematic research, a brief description of current work is given at the end of Lecture 8.

Persistence of patterns

If we return now to the patterns of attachment observed in one-year-olds, prospective studies show that each pattern of attachment, once developed, tends to persist. One reason for this is that the way a parent treats a child, whether for better or for worse, tends to continue unchanged. Another is that each pattern tends to be self-perpetuating. Thus a secure child is a happier and more rewarding child to care for and also is less demanding than an anxious one. An anxious ambivalent child is apt to be whiny and clinging; whilst an anxious avoidant child keeps his distance and is prone to bully other children. In both of these last cases the child's behaviour is likely to elicit an unfavourable response from the parent so that vicious circles develop.

Although for these reasons patterns, once formed, are apt to persist, this is by no means necessarily so. Evidence shows that during the first two or three years the pattern of attachment is a property of the relationship, for example, child to mother or child to father, and that if the parent treats the child differently the pattern will change accordingly. These changes are amongst much evidence reviewed by Sroufe (1985) that stability of pattern, when it occurs, cannot be attributed to the child's inborn temperament as has sometimes been claimed. Nevertheless, as a child grows older, the pattern becomes increasingly a property of the child himself, which means that he tends to impose it, or some derivative of it, upon new relationships such as with a teacher, a foster-mother, or a therapist.

The results of this process of internalization are evident in a prospective study which shows that the pattern of attachment characteristic of a mother-child pair, as assessed when the child is aged 12 months, is highly predictive of how that child will behave in a nursery group (with mother absent) three and a half years later. Thus children who showed a secure pattern with mother at 12 months are likely to be described by nursery staff as co-operative, popular with other children, resilient, and resourceful. Those who showed an anxious avoidant pattern are likely to be described as emotionally insulated, hostile or antisocial and, paradoxically, as unduly seeking of attention. Those who showed an anxious resistant pattern are likely to be described as also unduly seeking of attention and as either tense, impulsive, and easily frustrated or else as passive and helpless (Sroufe 1983). In view of these findings it is hardly surprising that in two other prospective studies, a pioneering one in California (Main and Cassidy 1988) and a replicative one in Germany (Wärtner 1986), the pattern of attachment assessed at 12 months is found to be highly predictive also of patterns of interaction with mother five years later.

Although the repertoire of a 6-year-old's behaviour towards a parent is vastly greater than that of a one-year-old, the earlier patterns of attachment are nonetheless readily discernible to an educated eye at the older age. Thus children who are classified as being securely attached at 6 years are those who treat their parents in a relaxed and friendly way, who enter into easy, and often subtle, intimacies with them, and who engage in free-flowing conversation. Children classified as anxious resistant show a mixture of insecurity, including sadness and fear, and of intimacy alternating with hostility, which is sometimes subtle and at others overt. In some of these cases the child's behaviour strikes an observer as self-conscious, even artificial. As though they were always anticipating a negative response from the parent, they try to ingratiate themselves by showing off, perhaps by being cute or especially charming (Main and Cassidy, in press; Main, personal communication).

Children aged 6 years classified as anxious avoidant tend quietly to keep the parent at a distance. Such greetings as they give are formal and brief; topics of conversation stay impersonal. He or she keeps busy with toys or some other activity and ignores or is even dismissive of a parent's initiatives.

Children who at 12 months appeared to be disorganized and/or disoriented are found five years later to be conspicuous for their tendency to control or dominate a parent. One form of this is to treat the parent in a humiliating and/or rejecting way; another is to be solicitous and protective. These are clear examples of what clinicians have labelled as an inversion, or reversal, of the child and parent roles. Conversations between them are fragmented, sentences begun but left unfinished, topics broached but changed abruptly.

In considering the persistence of a 6-year-old's patterns of interaction with parents and with other parental figures, a critical question arises: to what extent are the patterns at this age ingrained within the child's personality and to what extent are they a reflection of the way the parents still treat him or her? The answer, to which clinical experience points, is that by this age both these influences are at work so that the most effective interventions are those that take both into account, e.g. by means either of family therapy or else by giving help in parallel to parents and child.

As yet too little is known about how the influence on

personality development of interactions with the mother compares with the influence of those with the father. It would hardly be surprising were different facets of personality, manifest in different situations, to be influenced differently. In addition, their respective influences on males may be expected to differ from their respective influences on females. It is clearly a complex area that will require much research. Meanwhile it seems likely that, at least during the early years of an individual's life, the model of self interacting with mother is the more influential of the two. This would hardly be surprising since in every culture known the huge majority of infants and young children interact far more with the mother than with the father.

It must be recognized that, so far, prospective studies of the relative persistence of patterns of attachment, and of the features of personality characteristic of each, have not yet been carried beyond the sixth year. Even so, two cross-sectional studies of young adults show that the features of personality characteristic of each pattern during the early years are also to be found in young adults (Kobak and Sceery 1988; Cassidy and Kobak 1988; Hazan and Shaver 1987); and it is more than likely that, except in cases where family relations have changed substantially in the interval, they have been present continuously. All our clinical experience strongly supports that view.

A theory of internalization

In order to account for the tendency for patterns of attachment increasingly to become a property of the child himself, attachment theory invokes the concept of working models of self and of parents already described. The working models a child builds of his mother and her ways of communicating and behaving towards him, and a comparable model of his father, together with the complementary models of himself in interaction with each, are being built by a child during the first few years of his life and, it is postulated, soon become established as influential cognitive structures (Main, Kaplan, and Cassidy 1985). The forms they take, the evidence reviewed strongly suggests, are based on the child's real-life experience of day-to-day interactions

129

with his parents. Subsequently the model of himself that he builds reflects also the images that his parents have of him, images that are communicated not only by how each treats him but by what each *says* to him. These models then govern how he feels towards each parent and about himself, how he expects each of them to treat him, and how he plans his own behaviour towards them. They govern too both the fears and the wishes expressed in his day dreams.

Once built, evidence suggests, these models of a parent and self in interaction tend to persist and are so taken for granted that they come to operate at an unconscious level. As a securely attached child grows older and his parents treat him differently, a gradual up-dating of models occurs. This means that, though there is always a time-lag, his currently operative models continue to be reasonably good simulations of himself and his parents in interaction. In the case of the anxiously attached child, by contrast, this gradual up-dating of models is in some degree obstructed through defensive exclusion of discrepant experience and information. This means that the patterns of interaction to which the models lead, having become habitual, generalized, and largely unconscious, persist in a more or less uncorrected and unchanged state even when the individual in later life is dealing with persons who treat him in ways entirely unlike those that his parents adopted when he was a child.

The clue to an understanding of these differences in the degree to which models are up-dated is to be found in the profound differences in the freedom of communication between mother and child that characterize pairs of the two types. This is a variable to which Bretherton (1987) has drawn especial attention.

It will be noticed that in Main's longitudinal study described above the pattern of communication between a 6-year-old child and his mother, as observed in a pair that, five years earlier, had shown a secure pattern of attachment, is very different from that observed in a pair who had earlier shown an insecure pattern. Whereas the secure pairs engaged in free-flowing conversation laced with expressions of feeling, and touching on a variety of topics including personal ones, the insecure pairs did not. In some, conversation was fragmented and topics abruptly changed.

In others, notably the avoidant pairs, conversation was limited, topics kept impersonal, and all reference to feeling omitted. These striking differences in the degree to which communication is either free or restricted are postulated to be of great relevance for understanding why one child develops healthily and another becomes disturbed. Moreover it will not have escaped notice that this same variable, the degree to which communication between two individuals is restricted or relatively free, has for long been recognized as one of central concern in the practice of analytic psychotherapy.

For a relationship between any two individuals to proceed harmoniously each must be aware of the other's point-of-view, his goals, feelings, and intentions, and each must so adjust his own behaviour that some alignment of goals is negotiated. This requires that each should have reasonably accurate models of self and other which are regularly up-dated by free communication between them. It is here that the mothers of the securely attached children excel and those of the insecure are markedly deficient.

Once we focus on the degree to which communication between a parent–child pair is free-flowing or not, it quickly becomes apparent that, from the earliest days of life, the degree of freedom of communication in the pairs destined to develop a secure pattern of attachment is far greater than it is in those who do not (Ainsworth, Bell, and Stayton 1971; Blehar, Lieberman, and Ainsworth 1977). Thus it is characteristic of a mother whose infant will develop securely that she is continuously monitoring her infant's state and, as and when he signals wanting attention, she registers his signals and acts accordingly. By contrast, the mother of an infant later found to be anxiously attached is likely to monitor her infant's state only sporadically and, when she does notice his signals, to respond tardily and/or inappropriately. By the time an infant has reached his first birthday, moreover, these differences in freedom of communication have been found to be clearly evident during the Ainsworth Strange Situation procedure (Grossmann, Grossmann, and Schwan 1986). Even in the introductory episode, when infant and mother are alone together, more of the secure pairs were observed to engage in direct communication, by eye contact, facial expression, vocalization, and showing or giving toys, than did the insecure pairs. As the stress on the child increases, so do the differences between the pairs. Thus in the reunion episode after the second separation all but one of sixteen secure pairs communicated in direct fashion in contrast to a minority of the insecure ones. There was one other very striking difference moreover. Whereas every infant classified as secure was seen to be in direct communication with his mother, not only when he was content but also when he was distressed, the infants classified as avoidant, when they did engage in direct communication, did so only when they were content.

Thus already by the age of 12 months there are children who no longer express to their mothers one of their deepest emotions or the equally deep-seated desire for comfort and reassurance that accompanies it. It is not difficult to see what a very serious breakdown of communication between child and mother this represents. Not only that but, because a child's self-model is profoundly influenced by how his mother sees and treats him, whatever she fails to recognize in him he is likely to fail to recognize in himself. In this way, it is postulated, major parts of a child's developing personality can become split off from, that is, out of communication with, those parts of his personality that his mother recognizes and responds to, which in some cases include features of personality that she is attributing to him wrongly.

The upshot of this analysis is that obstruction to communication between different parts of, or systems within, a personality, which from the earliest days Freud saw as the crucial problem to be solved, is now seen as a reflection of the differential responses and communications of a mother to her child. When a mother responds favourably only to certain of her child's emotional communications and turns a blind eye or actively discourages others, a pattern is set for the child to identify with the favoured responses and to disown the others.

It is along these lines that attachment theory explains the differential development of resilient and mentally healthy personalities, and also of personalities prone to anxiety and depression, or to developing a false self or some other form of vulnerability to mental ill-health. Perhaps it is no coincidence that some of those who approach problems of personality development and psychopathology from a cognitive standpoint, but who also give weight to the power of emotion, e.g. Epstein (1980, 1986) and Liotti (1986, 1987), have been formulating theories that are essentially compatible with this one.

Variations in a mother's way of recalling her childhood experience

The conclusion so far reached about the role of free communication, emotional as well as cognitive, in determining mental health is strongly supported by an important recent finding from Main's longitudinal study. As a result of interviewing the mothers of the children in the study, Main found a strong correlation between how a mother describes her relationships with her parents during her childhood and the pattern of attachment her child now has with her (Main, Kaplan, and Cassidy 1985; see also Morris 1981 and Ricks 1985). Whereas the mother of a secure infant is able to talk freely and with feeling about her childhood, the mother of an insecure infant is not.

In this part of the study an interviewer asks the mother for a description of her early relationships and attachment-related events and for her sense of the way these relationships and events affected her personality. In considering results, as much or more attention is paid to the way a mother tells her story and deals with probing questions about it as to the historical material she describes. At the simplest level, it was found that a mother of a secure infant is likely to report having had a reasonably happy childhood and to show herself able to talk about it readily and in detail, giving due place to such unhappy events as may have occurred as well as to the happy ones. By contrast, a mother of an insecure infant is likely to respond to the enquiry in one of two different ways. One, shown by mothers of anxious resistant children, is to describe a difficult unhappy relationship with her own mother about which she is still clearly disturbed and in which she is still entangled mentally, and, should her mother be still alive, it is evident that she is entangled with her in reality as well. The other, shown by mothers of anxious avoidant children, is to claim in a generalized matter-of-fact way that she had a happy childhood, but not only is she unable to give any supporting detail but may refer to episodes pointing in an opposite direction. Frequently such a mother will insist that she can remember nothing about her childhood nor how she was treated. Thus the strong impression of clinicians, that a mother who had a happy childhood is likely to have a child who shows a secure attachment to her, and that an unhappy childhood, more or less cloaked by an inability to recall, makes for difficulties, is clearly supported.

Nevertheless a second finding, no less interesting and one of especial relevance here, arises from a study of the exceptions to the general rule. These are the mothers who describe having had a very unhappy childhood but who nonetheless have children showing secure attachment to them. A characteristic of each of these mothers, which distinguishes them from mothers of insecure infants, is that, despite describing much rejection and unhappiness during childhood, and perhaps tearful whilst doing so, each is able to tell her story in a fluent and coherent way, in which such positive aspects of her experiences as there were are given a due place and appear to have been integrated with all the negative ones. In their capacity for balance they resemble the other mothers of secure infants. It seemed to the interviewers and those assessing the transcripts that these exceptional mothers had thought much about their unhappy earlier experiences and how it had affected them in the long term, and also about why their parents might have treated them as they had. In fact, they seemed to have come to terms with their experience.

By contrast, the mothers of children whose pattern of attachment to them was insecure and who also described an unhappy childhood did so with neither fluency nor coherence: contradictions abounded and went unnoticed. Moreover, it was a mother who claimed an inability to recall her childhood and who did so both repeatedly and strongly who was a mother whose child was insecure in his relation to her.*

---

* In further examination of the data it has been found that all these correlations also hold true for fathers (Main, personal communication).

In the light of these findings Main and her colleagues conclude that free access to, and the coherent organization of information relevant to attachment play a determining role in the development of a secure personality in adult life. For someone who had a happy childhood no obstacles are likely to prevent free access to both the emotional and the cognitive aspects of such information. For someone who suffered much unhappiness or whose parents forbade him or her to notice or to remember adverse events, access is painful and difficult, and without help may indeed be impossible. Nevertheless, however she may accomplish it, when a woman manages either to retain or to regain access to such unhappy memories and reprocess them in such a way that she can come to terms with them, she is found to be no less able to respond to her child's attachment behaviour so that he develops a secure attachment to her than a woman whose childhood was a happy one. This is a finding to give great encouragement to the many therapists who for long have sought to help mothers in just this kind of way. Further reference to techniques for helping disturbed mothers is made at the end of Lecture 8.

Pathways to personality development

There is one further way in which attachment theory differs from traditional types of psychoanalytic theory, namely its rejection of the model of development in which an individual is held to pass through a series of stages in any one of which he may become fixated or to which he may regress, and its replacement by a model in which an individual is seen as progressing along one or another of an array of potential developmental pathways. Some of these pathways are compatible with healthy development; others deviate in one or another direction in ways incompatible with health.

All variants of the traditional model invoking phases of development are based on the assumption that, at some phase of normal development, a child shows psychological features that, in an older individual, would be regarded as signs of pathology. Thus a chronically anxious and clinging adult might be regarded as being fixated in or having regressed to a postulated phase of orality or of symbiosis; whilst a deeply withdrawn individual might be regarded as having regressed to a postulated phase of autism or of narcissism. Systematic and sensitive studies of human infants, such as those reported by Stern (1985), have now rendered this model untenable. Observations show that infants are socially responsive from birth onwards. Healthily developing toddlers do not show anxious clinging except when they are frightened or distressed; at other times they explore with confidence.

The model of developmental pathways regards an infant at birth as having an array of pathways potentially open to him, the one along which he will in fact proceed being determined at every moment by the interaction of the individual as he now is with the environment in which he happens then to be. Each infant is held to have his own individual array of potential pathways for personality development which, except for infants born with certain types of neurological damage, include many that are compatible with mental health and also many that are incompatible. Which particular pathway he proceeds along is determined by the environment he meets with, especially the way his parents (or parent substitutes) treat him, and how he responds to them. Children who have parents who are sensitive and responsive are enabled to develop along a healthy pathway. Those who have insensitive, unresponsive, neglectful, or rejecting parents are likely to develop along a deviant pathway which is in some degree incompatible with mental health and which renders them vulnerable to breakdown, should they meet with seriously adverse events. Even so, since the course of subsequent development is not fixed, changes in the way a child is treated can shift his pathway in either a more favourable direction or a less favourable one. Although the capacity for developmental change diminishes with age, change continues throughout the life cycle so that changes for better or for worse are always possible. It is this continuing potential for change that means that at no time of life is a person invulnerable to every possible adversity and also that at no time of life is a person impermeable to favourable influence. It is this persisting potential for change that gives opportunity for effective therapy.

136

LECTURE 8

Attachment, communication, and the therapeutic process

In the second part of my 1976 Maudsley Lecture, 'The making and breaking of affectional bonds' (1977), I described some of my ideas on the therapeutic implications of attachment theory. Much that has been learned since then has strengthened my confidence in the approach. The present account therefore should be regarded as an amplification of the earlier one. In it I give more detailed attention to the ways a patient's earlier experiences affect the transference relationship and discuss further the therapist's aim as being that of enabling his patient to reconstruct his working models of himself and his attachment figure(s) so that he becomes less under the spell of forgotten miseries and better able to recognize companions in the present for what they are.

a thing which has not been understood
inevitably reappears; like an unlaid ghost,
it cannot rest until the mystery has been
resolved and the spell broken.

Sigmund Freud 1909

Those who cannot remember the past are
condemned to repeat it.

George Santayana 1905

Five therapeutic tasks

The theory of personality development and psychopathology outlined above can be used as a framework to guide each one of the three principal forms of analytic psychotherapy in use today – individual therapy, family therapy, and group therapy. Here I deal only with the first.

A therapist applying attachment theory sees his role as being one of providing the conditions in which his patient can explore his representational models of himself and his attachment figures with a view to reappraising and restructuring them in the light of the new understanding he acquires and the new experiences he has in the therapeutic relationship. In helping his patient towards this end the therapist's role can be described under five main heads.

The first is to provide the patient with a secure base from which he can explore the various unhappy and painful aspects of his life, past and present, many of which he finds it difficult or perhaps impossible to think about and reconsider without a trusted companion to provide support, encouragement, sympathy, and, on occasion, guidance.

A second is to assist the patient in his explorations by encouraging him to consider the ways in which he engages in relationships with significant figures in his current life, what his expectations are for his own feelings and behaviour and for those of other people, what unconscious biases he may be bringing when he selects a person with whom he hopes to make an intimate relationship and when he creates situations that go badly for him.

A particular relationship that the therapist encourages the patient to examine, and that constitutes the third task, is the relationship between the two of them. Into this the patient will import all those perceptions, constructions, and expectations of how an attachment figure is likely to feel and behave towards him that his working models of parents and self dictate.

A fourth task is to encourage the patient to consider how his current perceptions and expectations and the feelings and actions to which they give rise may be the product either of the events and situations he encountered during his childhood and adolescence, especially those with his parents, or else as the products of what he may repeatedly have been told by them. This is often a painful and difficult process and not infrequently requires that the therapist sanction his patient to consider as possibilities ideas and feelings about his parents that he has hitherto regarded as unimaginable and unthinkable. In doing so a patient may find himself moved by strong emotions and urges to action, some directed towards his parents and some towards the therapist, and many of which he finds frightening and/or alien and unacceptable.

The therapist's fifth task is to enable his patient to recognize that his images (models) of himself and of others, derived either from past painful experiences or from misleading messages emanating from a parent, but all too often in the literature mislabelled as 'fantasies', may or may not be appropriate to his present and future; or, indeed, may never have been justified. Once he has grasped the nature of his governing images (models) and has traced their origins, he may begin to understand what has led him to see the world and himself as he does and so to feel, to think, and to act in the ways he does. He is then in a position to reflect on the accuracy and adequacy of those images (models), and on the ideas and actions to which they lead, in the light of his current experiences of emotionally significant people, including the therapist as well as his parents, and of himself in relationship to each. Once the process has started he begins to see the old images (models) for what they are, the not unreasonable products of his past experiences or of what he has repeatedly been told, and thus to feel free to imagine alternatives better fitted to his current life. By these means the therapist hopes to enable his patient to cease being a slave to old and unconscious stereotypes and to feel, to think, and to act in new ways.

Readers will be aware that the principles set out have a great deal in common with the principles described by other analytically trained psychotherapists who regard conflicts arising within interpersonal relationships as the key to an understanding of their patient's problems, who focus on the transference and who also give some weight, albeit of varying degree, to a patient's earlier experience with his parents.

A Secure Base

Among the many well-known names that could be mentioned in this context are those of Fairbairn, Winnicott, and Guntrip in Britain, and Sullivan, Fromm-Reichmann, Gill, and Kohut in the United States. Among recently published works that contain many of the ideas prescribed here are those by Peterfreund (1983), Casement (1985), Pine (1985), and Strupp and Binder (1984), and also those of Malan (1973) and Horowitz *et al.* (1984) in the field of brief psychotherapy. In particular, I wish to draw attention to the ideas of Horowitz and his colleagues who, in their description of the treatment of patients suffering from an acute stress syndrome, employ a conceptual framework closely similar to that presented here. Although their technique is aimed to help patients recover from the effects of a recent severely stressful event, I believe the principles informing their work are equally applicable to helping patients recover from the effects of a chronic disturbance resulting from stressful events of many years ago, including those that occurred during their earliest years.

Although in this exposition it is convenient to list the therapist's five tasks in a logical way, so interrelated are they that in practice a productive session is likely to involve first one task, then another. Nevertheless, unless a therapist can enable his patient to feel some measure of security, therapy cannot even begin. Thus we start with the role of the therapist in providing his patient with a secure base. This is a role very similar to that described by Winnicott as 'holding' and by Bion as 'containing'.

In providing his patient with a secure base from which to explore and express his thoughts and feelings the therapist's role is analogous to that of a mother who provides her child with a secure base from which to explore the world. The therapist strives to be reliable, attentive, and sympathetically responsive to his patient's explorations and, so far as he can, to see and feel the world through his patient's eyes, namely to be empathic. At the same time he is aware that, because of his patient's adverse experiences in the past, the patient may not believe that the therapist is to be trusted to behave kindly or to understand his predicament. Alternatively the unexpectedly attentive and sympathetic responses the patient receives may lead him to

140

suppose that the therapist will provide him with all the care and affection which he has always yearned for but never had. In the one case therefore the therapist is seen in an unduly critical and hostile light, in the other as ready to provide more than is at all realistic. Since, it is held, both types of misunderstanding and misconstruction, and the emotions and behaviour to which they give rise, are central features of the patient's troubles, a therapist needs to have the widest possible knowledge of the many forms these misconstructions can take and also of the many types of earlier experience from which they are likely to have sprung. Without such knowledge a therapist is poorly placed to see and feel the world as his patient is doing.

Even so, a patient's way of construing his relationship with his therapist is not determined solely by the patient's history: it is determined no less by the way the therapist treats him. Thus the therapist must strive always to be aware of the nature of his own contribution to the relationship which, amongst other influences, is likely to reflect in one way or another what he experienced himself during his own childhood. This aspect of therapy, the counter-transference, is a big issue of its own and the subject of a large literature. Since it is not possible to deal with it further here, I want to emphasize not only the importance of the counter-transference but also that the focus of therapy must always be on the interactions of patient and therapist in the here and now, and that the only reason for encouraging the patient at times to explore his past is for the light it throws on his current ways of feeling and dealing with life.

With that proviso firmly in mind, let us consider some of the commoner forms that a patient's misconstructions can take and how they are likely to have originated. This is the aspect of therapy in which the work of a therapist who adopts attachment theory is likely to differ most from one who adopts certain of the traditional theories of personality development and psychopathology. Thus, for example, a therapist who views his patient's misperceptions and misunderstandings as the not unreasonable products of what the patient has actually experienced in the past, or has repeatedly been told, differs sharply from one who sees these same misperceptions and misunderstandings as the irrational offspring of autonomous and unconscious fantasy.

In what follows I am drawing on several distinct sources of information: studies by epidemiologists; the studies by developmental psychologists already referred to; observations made during the course of family therapy; and not least what I have learned from patients whom I have treated myself and from those whose therapy I have supervised.

Influence of earlier experiences on the transference relationship

It not infrequently happens that a patient is acutely apprehensive lest his therapist reject, criticize, or humiliate him. Since we know that all too many children are treated in this way by one or other, or both, of their parents, we can be reasonably confident that that has been our patient's experience. Should it seem likely that the patient is aware of how he is feeling and how he expects the therapist to treat him, the therapist will indicate that he also is aware of the problem. How soon the therapist can link these expectations to the patient's experiences of his parents, in the present perhaps as well as the past, turns on how willing the patient is to consider that possibility, or whether, by contrast, he insists that his parents' treatment of him is above criticism. Where the latter situation obtains, there is the prior problem of trying to understand why the patient should insist on retaining this favourable picture when such evidence as is available points to its being mistaken.

It happens in some families that one or other parent insists that he or she is an admirable parent who has always done everything possible for the child and that, in so far as friction is present, the fault lies exclusively with the child. This attitude of the parent all too often cloaks behaviour that, by ordinary standards, has been far from perfect. Yet, since the parent insists that he or she has given the child constant affection and that the child must have been born bad and ungrateful, the child has little option but to accept the picture, despite being aware somewhere in his mind that the picture is hardly fair.

An added complication arises when a patient has, as a child, been subjected to the strongest of instructions from a parent on no account to tell anyone of certain happenings within the family. These are usually quarrels in which the parent is aware that his or her behaviour is open to criticism; for example, quarrels between the parents, or between a parent and a child, during which dreadful things have been said or done. The more insistent a therapist is that his patient tell everything, the more distressing the dilemma is for his patient. Injunctions to silence are not uncommon in families and have been much neglected as sources of what has traditionally been called resistance. It is often useful for a therapist to enquire of a patient whether he may have been subjected to such pressures and, if so, to help him resolve the dilemma.

So far we have been considering cases in which a patient is in some degree aware of his expectations of being rejected, criticized, or humiliated. Not infrequently, however, a patient seems wholly unaware of any such feelings despite his attitude to the therapist exuding distrust and evasion. Evidence shows that these states of mind occur especially in those who, having developed an anxiously avoidant pattern of attachment during early years, have striven ever since to be emotionally self-contained and insulated against intimate contacts with other people. These patients, who are often described as being narcissistic or as having a false self, avoid therapy as long as they can and, should they undertake it, keep the therapist at arm's length. If allowed to, some will talk incessantly about anything and everything except emotionally charged relationships, past or present. Others will explain that they have nothing to talk about. One young woman, whose every move indicated deep distrust of me, spent the time boasting of her delinquent exploits, many of them fictitious I suspected, and pouring contempt on what she insisted was my dull and narrow life. To treat such deeply distrustful people was compared many years ago by Adrian Stephen (1934) with trying to make friends with a shy or frightened pony: both situations require a prolonged, quiet, and friendly patience. Only when the therapist is aware of the constant rebuffs the patient is likely to have been subjected to as a child whenever he sought comfort or help, and of his terror of being subjected to something similar from the therapist, can the latter see the situation between them as his patient is seeing it.

Another and quite different cause of wariness of any close contact with a therapist for the patient is dread lest the therapist trap him into a relationship aimed to serve the therapist's interests rather than his own. A common origin of such fear is a childhood in which a parent, almost always mother, has sought to make the child her own attachment figure and caregiver, that is, has inverted the relationship. Very often this is done unconsciously and using techniques that, to an uninformed eye, may appear to be overindulgence but that are really bribes to retain the child in a caregiving role.

Not infrequently a patient shifts during the therapy from treating his therapist as though he was one or other of his parents to behaving towards him in the way one of his parents had treated him. For example, a patient who has been subjected to hostile threats as a child may use hostile threats to his therapist. Experiences of scornful contempt from a parent may be re-enacted as scornful contempt of the therapist. Sexual advances from a parent may reappear as sexual advances to the therapist. Such behaviour may be understood in the following way. During his childhood a person learns two principal forms of behaviour and builds in his mind two principal types of model. One form of behaviour is, of course, that of a child, namely himself, interacting with a parent, his mother or his father. The corresponding working models he builds are those of himself as a child in interaction with each parent. The other form of behaviour is that of a parent, namely his mother or his father, interacting with a child, himself. The corresponding models he builds are those of each parent in interaction with himself. Therefore, whenever a therapist is puzzled by, or resentful of, the way he is being treated by a patient, he is always wise to enquire when and from whom the patient may have learned that way of treating other people. More often than not it is from one of his parents.*

---

* Within traditional theory this shift of role by a patient is likely to be termed a case of identification with the aggressor.

With some patients the therapeutic relationship is one in which anxiety, distrust, and criticism, and sometimes also anger and contempt, are overt and predominate, and the therapist seen in dark colours. Such sentiments as gratitude for the therapist's efforts or respect for his competence are conspicuous by their absence. The task then is to help the patient grasp that much of his present resentment stems from past mistreatment at the hands of others and that, however understandable his anger may be as a result, to continue fighting old battles is unproductive. To accept that an unhappy past cannot be changed is usually a bitter pill.

With other patients the situation is reversed: the transference relationship becomes one in which overt gratitude, admiration, and affection are readily expressed, and the therapist seen in a glow of rosy perfection. Dissatisfaction and criticism are notably absent, and anger at the therapist's shortcomings, especially absences, unimaginable. Such idealization of the therapist springs, I believe, partly from unrealistic hopes and expectations of what the therapist is able and willing to provide, and partly from a childhood in which criticism of a parent is forbidden and compliance enforced, either by some guilt-inducing technique or else by sanctions such as threats not to love, or even to abandon, the child. With this type of childhood experience, the patient's unconscious assumption is that the therapist will expect the same degree of obedience as his parents had expected and will enforce it by techniques or by threats similar to the ones they used.

Unfortunately there has been a tendency in some quarters to confuse the theory advanced here, which regards the way certain parents treat their children as being a major cause of mental ill-health, with an attitude of mind that simply blames parents. No one who works in the fields of child psychiatry and family therapy is likely to make this mistake. On the contrary, as already remarked, it has long been recognized that the misguided behaviour of parents is more often than not the product of their own difficult and unhappy childhood. As a result much skilled time has always been devoted to helping parents escape from the adverse influences of their own childhoods.

145

Furthermore, during the treatment of an individual (of any age) who has suffered at the hands of his parents, the therapist, whilst accepting the patient's account, avoids moral judgement. On the contrary, whenever opportunity offers, he will encourage his patient to consider how and why the parent under discussion may have behaved as he or she has done. In raising these questions, it is always useful for the therapist to enquire of the patient what he knows of the childhood experiences that the parent in question may have had. Not infrequently this leads the patient to gain some understanding of how things had developed and, from understanding, often to move on to a measure of forgiveness and reconciliation. In family sessions it can be especially valuable if a parent can be encouraged to give an account of his or her childhood. This enables all those present – the parent him- or herself, the spouse, the children, and the therapist – to gain some insight into how and why family life has developed as it has and how each can best help improve it. As already mentioned (p. 133), this strong tendency for attachment problems to be transmitted across generations, through the influence on parenting behaviour of relationship problems stemming from the parent's own childhood, is at last receiving the research attention it deserves.

Some pathogenic situations and events of childhood

A therapist, I believe, cannot be too well informed about the disguised and distorted relationships that can occur in some families, and the terrible things that can happen in others, for it is only if he is so informed that he can have a reasonably clear idea of what probably lies behind his patient's defences, or of the origins of his anxiety, anger, and guilt. Once he is adequately informed, he is well placed not only to appreciate the truth of what his patient may be describing as having happened to him but also to broach, more or less tentatively, some of the kinds of situation to which the patient may well have been exposed but to which he may be either unable or unwilling to refer. In listing the following situations I am doing no more than indicating some that are both common and have, until recently, been neglected in the psychotherapeutic literature.*

Threats not to love a child used as a means of control

It is easy for a mother to say to a child that she will not love him if he behaves in such and such a way. What this means is that the mother is threatening not to provide affection or comfort at times when her child is upset, frightened, or distressed, and not to provide help or encouragement at other times. If such threats are used systematically by either parent, or both, the child inevitably grows up intensely anxious to please and guilt-prone.

Threats to abandon a child

Threats to abandon are a degree more frightening to a child than threats no longer to love him. This is especially so if the parent enacts a threat, perhaps by disappearing herself for a few hours or by packing her child's suitcase and walking him up the street, allegedly to the home for bad boys. Since threats to abandon often take a highly idiosyncratic form, a patient may deny that he was ever subjected to them. In such cases the truth may emerge with its accompanying emotion only when the special way in which the threat was phrased is recollected. One example is a mother who had concocted the story that a yellow van would draw up and take her son away. Another is a father whose story was that his daughter would be sent to a school on a remote rock surrounded by sharks (Marrone 1984). Thus, in the first case, all the mother had to say was 'Well the yellow van will come', and, in the second, for the father to say 'Then it will be the rock school', for the child instantly to desist from whatever he or she was doing. In a third case, the code word was 'margarine', the mother having coupled her threat to send her son away to a children's home with an insistence that he would have to eat margarine there. For these patients a general phrase

---

* Since in previous publications I have given much attention to the ill effects on personality development of bereavements and prolonged separations, these themes are omitted from what follows.

like 'threat to abandon' had failed to ring a bell. Only when the code word was unearthed was the original terror experienced afresh and the source of the separation anxiety located.

Threats to commit suicide

Sometimes a distraught parent threatens to commit suicide if some distressing situation continues. This may occur during quarrels between parents, which the child overhears, or may be directed at the child himself. In either case such threats strike terror. One lesson to be learned from these cases is that, whenever a patient refers to his parents as having quarrelled, the therapist should always enquire 'What did they *say* to each other?' Not infrequently a patient blocks at this. In a fit of temper quarrelling parents may say appalling things to each other. This is bad enough. What makes it far worse is when, after cooling down, they disclaim having said any such thing.

Disclaimers and disconfirmations

Examples of disclaimers by a parent of what he or she has said or done, and persistent efforts to disconfirm what a child has seen or heard, are given in some detail in Lecture 6 and the adverse effects on personality development of such pressures emphasized. During therapy these effects emerge as great uncertainty in a patient as to whether some family episode did or did not occur and guilt about adumbrating it. Here, as so often, a key role for the therapist is to sanction the patient's exploration of all the various possibilities, both those favourable to his parents and those unfavourable to them, and to encourage him to weigh the evidence available, whilst he (the therapist) remains resolutely open-minded as to where the truth may lie.

Thus far in this exposition I have not considered the critical issue of how far we can and should rely on the validity of our patients' reports. Memories are certainly fallible, and there are various occasions when an experienced therapist will rightly question the truth of what his patient is saying. What then are the criteria by which we should judge?

First, broad generalizations about the kind of parent the mother or father was and about the kind of parenting received are never to be given credence unless and until they are supported by detailed examples of how each treated the patient as a child in particular situations. For example, the glowing account of a wonderful mother may well go unsupported when detail becomes available. Valid accounts of affectionate parenting not only give plenty of favourable details but are likely also to be interlaced with occasional criticism, so that the parent can be seen in the round. Similarly, disparaging accounts of parents in uniformly adverse terms need close examination. Invalid accounts of either sort tend to be sweeping and extreme, to be either white or black. Detail is either lacking or, should it be given, is at variance with the portrait presented. By contrast, whenever plenty of consistent detail is given and the picture that emerges conforms to what we know, from other sources, does happen in other families, and also to the known antecedents of the types of problem besetting the patient, it is absurd to doubt its overall validity, even if some points remain in question.

The origin of these extremes is not infrequently external pressure. For example, one parent has insisted that the child take sides with him or her against the other parent who is represented as being all bad. Or else a parent who has many shortcomings insists that he or she is above criticism.

Another occasion when a therapist is right to doubt the patient's story is when there is reason to suspect that the patient is a pathological liar. Such cases are comparatively rare and, if only for that reason, may go undetected for a time. Sooner or later, however, mounting inconsistencies and improbabilities, as well as the way the patient tells his story, engender first doubt and, later, certainty that the patient is not to be believed.

Apart from these exceptions I believe patients' accounts are sufficiently trustworthy that a therapist should accept them as being reasonable approximations to the truth;* and furthermore that it is anti-therapeutic not to do so. Constantly to query the

---

* For research purposes, however, criteria for accepting retrospective information as valid must be much stricter.

validity of the patient's story, even if only by implication, and insistence on the distorting role of imagination or fantasy, is the reverse of empathic. It conveys to the patient that the therapist does not understand him and may indeed convince him that the therapist is behaving exactly as his parent had predicted. Thus some parents, having insisted that their child not tell of something the parent is ashamed of, may then add that, in any case, were he to do so no one would believe him.

Among the large range of adverse events and situations not so far mentioned in this lecture that a therapist should have in his mind as likely to have occurred in the life of one patient or another are the following:

a child may never have been wanted by one or both parents;

a child may be of the wrong sex in a family in which parents had set their hearts on a boy or a girl;

a child may have been made the family scapegoat, sometimes as a result of a family tragedy that, with greater or less plausibility, has always been attributed to him;

a parent may have used guilt-inducing techniques to control a child, for example, frequent claims that the child's behaviour makes mother ill;

a parent may have sought to make one of her children her attachment figure by discouraging him from exploring the world away from her and from believing that he will ever be able to make his way on his own;

a child's unusual role in a family may be the result of his mother having had an extra-marital affair during her marriage so that the child's putative father is not his real father;

another cause of a child's unusual role is when one or other parent identifies one child with a relative, often one of the child's grandparents, with whom he or she has had a difficult relationship, and who then re-enacts that relationship with the child;

a child may have been the target of more or less serious physical abuse from a parent or step-parent;

a child may have been involved in sexual abuse from a parent, step-parent, or older sibling for short or long periods of time.

For those unaware of the commoner effects on personality development of exposure to situations of these kinds, a number of references are given in an Appendix (pp. 173–4).

Inevitably the influential events of an individual's first two or three years will either never have been registered in his memory or else cannot now be recalled. Here, of course, the best a therapist can do is to infer, on the basis of the transference situation and of such information as the patient has gleaned about his early years, combined with such wider knowledge of personality development as the therapist has acquired, what the nature of those events may have been. In other words, he resorts to reconstruction; but in doing so he can in future draw on a much wider and more reliable knowledge of family influences on personality development than has traditionally been available to analytically trained psychotherapists.

The therapist's stance

In this account of therapeutic principles, therapists will recognize much that has long been familiar, though often under a different name. The therapeutic alliance appears as a secure base, an internal object as a working, or representational, model of an attachment figure, reconstruction as exploring memories of the past, resistance (sometimes) as deep reluctance to disobey the past orders of parents not to tell or not to remember. Among points of difference is the emphasis placed on the therapist's role as a companion for his patient in the latter's exploration of himself and his experiences, and less on the therapist interpreting things to the patient. Whilst some traditional therapists might be described as adopting the stance 'I know; I'll tell you', the stance I advocate is one of 'You know, you tell me'. Thus the patient is encouraged to believe that, with support and occasional guidance, he can discover for himself the true nature of the models that underlie his thoughts, feelings, and actions and that, by examining the nature of his earlier experiences with his parents, or parent substitutes, he will understand what has led him to build the models now active within him and thus be free to restructure them. Fortunately the human psyche, like human bones, is strongly inclined towards self-healing. The psychotherapist's job, like that of the orthopaedic surgeon's, is to provide the conditions in which self-healing can best take place.

Amongst those who have recently given detailed accounts of the special value of adopting a modest and tentative approach are Peterfreund (1983) and Casement (1985).

In the foregoing description the therapist's role has been likened to that of a mother who provides her child with a secure base from which to explore. This means, first and foremost, that he accepts and respects his patient, warts and all, as a fellow human being in trouble and that his over-riding concern is to promote his patient's welfare by all means at his disposal. To this end the therapist strives to be reliable, attentive, empathic, and sympathetically responsive, and also to encourage his patient to explore the world of his thoughts, feelings, and actions not only in the present but also in the past. Whilst always encouraging his patient to take the initiative, the therapist is in no sense passive. On the one hand he tries to be attentive and sensitively responsive. On the other, he recognizes that there are times when he himself should take the initiative. For example, when a patient wastes time talking about everything and anything except his thoughts and feelings about people, it will be necessary to draw his attention to his avoidance of the area, and perhaps also to his deep distrust of the therapist's efforts to be helpful or of his capacity to keep confidences. With another patient, who perhaps is very willing to explore memories of childhood, there will be many occasions when a therapist can usefully ask for more detail or raise questions about situations of childhood that the patient has so far not referred to directly, but which seem plausible possibilities in the light of what he has been describing, and in the light also of the particular problems from which the patient is suffering. In doing so, moreover, the therapist must never forget that his patient may still be strongly influenced by his parents' injunctions not to know about events he is not supposed to know about and not to experience feelings he is not supposed to experience.

An interruption to therapy probably always generates some reaction in a patient; sometimes it is conscious, at others unconscious, but nonetheless evident. When conscious, it may take the form of overt complaint or angry protest; when unconscious it may manifest itself by the patient disparaging therapy or missing a session or two before the break. How a therapist evaluates these reactions and responds to them will reflect his theoretical position. Someone who adopts attachment theory will respect his patient's distress or anger about the separation and will regard them as the natural responses of someone who has become attached to another – a respect that will be implicit in anything he says or does. At the same time he will give attention to the form his patient's reaction takes. If openly expressed, he will be sympathetic and may be able to ease the patient's distress by giving him information about how he could communicate during the break. In addition, the therapist will consider how the patient is construing the interruption and, should there be evidence of misconstruction, will attempt to discover how it may have originated. If, for example, the patient is apprehensive that the therapist will not return, the possibility of the patient having been exposed to threats by a parent to abandon him might be explored. In cases where the interruption is due to the therapist being unwell, he will be alert to the possibility that the patient may be apprehensive lest something he (the patient) has done or said is responsible. Were that to be so, the therapist would explore whether one of the patient's parents had sought to control him by claiming that the way he behaved was making mother or father ill.

Similarly, should a patient react to an interruption by disparaging therapy or missing a session, a therapist who adopts attachment theory would ask himself why his patient is afraid to express his feelings openly and what his childhood experiences may have been to account for his distrust.

It is not unlikely that the description just given of a therapist's mode of responding to his patient's reactions to an interruption will contrast with that of a therapist who adopts and applies one or another of the traditional psychoanalytic theories. For example, one such therapist might regard his patient's reactions as being rather childish, even infantile, and as indicating that the patient was fixated in an oral or a symbiotic phase. What the therapist then might say, and especially the way he might say it, could well be experienced by the patient as lacking in respect for his (the patient's) current feelings of attachment, distress, or anger. Here again there would be danger that the therapist might appear to be responding in a cold unsympathetic way and all too like one or other of the patient's parents. Were that so the exchange would be anti-therapeutic.

How far a therapist can wisely go in meeting a patient's desire to keep in communication during breaks, e.g. by telephone, and for comforting when distressed during a session, turns on many personal factors in their relationship. On the one hand, there is danger of the therapist's appearing to lack sympathy for the patient's distress or even to seem rejecting. On the other is the risk of his appearing to offer more than he is prepared to give. There are occasions when it would be inhuman not to allow a distressed patient to make some form of physical contact: the roles are then explicitly comforter and comforted. Yet there is always danger that physical contact can elicit sexual feelings, especially when sexes are different. Depending on the situation each therapist must make his own decisions and draw his own lines. The more alive to such issues a therapist is the better will he be able to avoid the pitfalls.

Emotional communications and the restructuring of working models

When a therapist utilizes the kind of technique advocated here, it can sometimes happen that therapy gets into a rut in which the patient persists endlessly in describing what a terrible time he had as a child and how badly his parents treated him, without any progress being made. One cause of such perseveration, I suspect, is that the patient is convinced that his therapist does not accept the truth of what he is saying: hence his endless repetition of it. This may be due to the patient having always been scoffed at by those to whom he has told the story in the past or, and perhaps more commonly, to the therapist himself having indicated scepticism or disbelief. This can be done in a myriad of ways, by tone of voice, by querying the details, by failing to attach any particular weight to what the patient describes.

Evidently when the problem lies in the therapist's incredulity the way out is for him to make it plain that he knows all too well that such things do happen to children and has no reason to doubt the patient's account. Even so the impasse may continue: the story is told and retold in a flat cynical way with no show of feeling whatever.

This situation has been discussed by Selma Fraiberg who, with colleagues, set out to help vulnerable mothers at risk of either neglecting or abusing their infants (Fraiberg, Adelson, and Shapiro 1975). They describe making visits to the homes of two such mothers and listening to the distressing tales these women had to tell. Each told a story of gross cruelty during childhood – being subjected to violent beatings, being locked out in the cold, often deserted by mother, being shunted from one place to another, and of having no one to go to for help or comfort. Neither gave a hint of how they might have *felt* nor what they may have felt like *doing*. One, a girl of sixteen who avoided touching or holding her baby (who screamed hopelessly), insisted: 'But what's the use of talking? I always kept things to myself. I want to forget. I don't want to think.' This was the point at which the therapist intervened – by herself expressing all the feelings that any and every child would be expected to have in the situations described: how frightened, how angry, how hopeless one would feel, and also how one *would long to go to someone* who would understand and provide comfort and protection. In doing so the therapist not only showed an understanding of how the patient must have felt, but communicated in her manner that the expression of such feeling and desire would be met with a sympathetic and comforting response. . Only then was it possible for the young mother to express all the grief, the tears, 'and the unspeakable anguish for herself as a cast-off child' that she had always felt but had never dared express.

155

In this account of Fraiberg's methods of helping a patient express the emotions she dares not show I have deliberately emphasized the link between emotion and action. Failure to express emotion is due very largely to unconscious fear lest the action of which the emotion is a part will lead to a dreaded outcome. In many families anger with an adult leads to punishment which can sometimes be severe. Moreover a tearful appeal for comfort and help can lead to rejection and humiliation. It is perhaps too often forgotten by clinicians that many children, when they become distressed and weepy and are looking for comfort, are shooed off as intolerable little cry-babies. Instead of the comforting provided by an understanding and affectionate parent, these children meet with an unsympathetic and critical rebuff. No wonder therefore if, should this pattern prevail during childhood, the child learns never to show distress or seek comfort and, should he undertake therapy, assumes that his therapist will be as intolerant of anger and tears as his parents always were.

Every therapist who adopts a psychoanalytic perspective has long recognized that, to be effective, therapy requires that a patient not only talks about his memories, his ideas and dreams, his hopes and desires, but also expresses his feelings. The discussion of Fraiberg's technique for helping a cynical and frozen young woman to discover the depth of her feelings and to express them freely to her therapist is therefore a fitting note on which to end.

In writing this lecture I have throughout been aware that, by using terms such as 'information', 'communication', and 'working models', it would be easy for an unwary reader to suppose that these terms belong within a psychology concerned only with cognition and one bereft of feeling and action. Although for many years it was all too common for cognitive psychologists to omit reference to emotion, it is now recognized that to do so is artificial and unfruitful (Hinde, Perret-Clermont, and Stevenson-Hinde 1985). There are, in fact, no more important communications between one human being and another than those expressed emotionally, and no information more vital for constructing and reconstructing working models of self and other than information about how each feels towards the other. During the earliest years of our lives, indeed, emotional expression and its reception are the only means of communication we have, so that the foundations of our working models of self and attachment figure are perforce laid using information from that source alone. Small wonder therefore, if, in reviewing his attachment relationships during the course of psychotherapy and restructuring his working models, it is the emotional communications between a patient and his therapist that play the crucial part.

References

Adams-Tucker, C. (1982) 'Proximate effects of sexual abuse in child-hood: a report on 28 children', *American Journal of Psychiatry*, 139: 1252–6.

Ainsworth, M.D. (1962) 'The effects of maternal deprivation: a review of findings and controversy in the context of research strategy' in: *Deprivation of maternal care: a reassessment of its effects*, Public Health Papers no. 14, Geneva: World Health Organisation.

Ainsworth, M.D. (1963) 'The development of infant–mother interaction among the Ganda' in B. M. Foss (ed.) *Determinants of infant behaviour*, vol. 2, London: Methuen; New York: Wiley.

Ainsworth, M.D.S. (1967) *Infancy in Uganda: infant care and the growth of attachment* Baltimore: Johns Hopkins University Press.

Ainsworth, M.D.S. (1969) 'Object relations, dependency and attach-ment: a theoretical review of the infant-mother relationship', *Child Development*, 40: 969–1025.

Ainsworth, M.D.S. (1977) 'Social development in the first year of life: maternal influences on infant–mother attachment' in J. M. Tanner (ed.) *Developments in psychiatric research*, London: Tavistock.

Ainsworth, M.D.S. (1982) 'Attachment: retrospect and prospect' in C.M. Parkes and J. Stevenson-Hinde (eds) *The place of attachment in human behavior*, 3–30, New York: Basic Books; London: Tavistock.

Ainsworth, M.D.S. (1985) 'I Patterns of infant-mother attachment: antecedents and effects on development' and 'II Attachments across the life-span', *Bulletin of New York Academy of Medicine*, 61: 771–91 and 791–812.

Ainsworth, M.D.S. and Wittig, B.A. (1969) 'Attachment and explora-

References

tory behaviour of one-year-olds in a strange situation' in B.M. Foss (ed.) *Determinants of infant behaviour*, vol. 4, London: Methuen; New York: Barnes & Noble.

Ainsworth, M.D.S., Bell, S.M., and Stayton, D.J. (1971) 'Individual differences in strange situation behavior of one-year-olds' in H.R. Schaffer (ed.) *The origins of human social relations*, 17–57, London: Academic Press.

Ainsworth, M.D., Blehar, M.C., Waters, E., and Wall, S. (1978) *Patterns of attachment: assessed in the strange situation and at home*, Hillsdale, NJ: Lawrence Erlbaum.

Anderson, J.W. (1972) 'Attachment behaviour out of doors' in N. Blurton Jones (ed). *Ethological studies of child behaviour*, Cambridge: Cambridge University Press.

Arend, R., Gove, F.L., and Sroufe, L.A. (1979) 'Continuity of individual adaptation from infancy to kindergarten: a predictive study of ego-resiliency and curiosity in preschoolers', *Child Development*, 50: 950–9.

Baldwin, J. (1977) 'Child abuse: epidemiology and prevention' in *Epidemiological approaches in child psychiatry*, 55–106, London: Academic Press.

Ballou, J. (1978) 'The significance of reconciliative themes in the psychology of pregnancy', *Bulletin of the Menninger Clinic*, 42: 383–413.

Bender, L. (1947) 'Psychopathic behaviour disorders in children' in R.M. Lindner and R.V. Seliger (eds) *Handbook of correctional psychology*, New York: Philosophical Library.

Bender, L. and Yarnell, H. (1941) 'An observation nursery', *American Journal of Psychiatry*, 97: 1158–74.

Blehar, M.C., Lieberman, A.F., and Ainsworth, M.D.S. (1977) 'Early face-to-face interaction and its relations to later infant–mother attachment', *Child Development*, 48: 182–94.

Blight, J.G. (1981) 'Must psychoanalysis retreat to hermeneutics?', *Psychoanalysis and Contemporary Thought*, 4: 147–205.

Bliss, E.L. (1980) 'Multiple personalities: report of 14 cases with implications for schizophrenia and hysteria', *Archives of General Psychiatry*, 37: 1388–97.

Bliss, E.L. (1986) *Multiple personality, allied disorders and hypnosis*, Oxford: Oxford University Press.

Bloch, D. (1978) *'So the witch won't eat me'*, Boston: Houghton Mifflin.

Bowlby, J. (1940) 'The influence of early environment in the development of neurosis and neurotic character', *International Journal of Psycho-Analysis*, 21: 154–78.

Bowlby, J. (1944) 'Forty-four juvenile thieves: their characters and home life', *International Journal of Psycho-Analysis*, 25: 19–52 and 107–27.

Bowlby, J. (1951) *Maternal care and mental health*, Geneva: World Health Organisation; London: Her Majesty's Stationery Office; New York: Columbia University Press; abridged version: *Child Care and the Growth of Love* (second edn, 1965) Harmondsworth: Penguin.

Bowlby, J. (1958) The nature of the child's tie to his mother, *International Journal of Psycho-Analysis, 39*: 350–73.

Bowlby, J. (1960) 'Grief and mourning in infancy and early childhood', *The Psychoanalytic Study of the Child*, 15: 9–52.

Bowlby, J. (1961) 'Processes of mourning', *International Journal of Psycho-Analysis*, 42: 317–40.

Bowlby, J. (1969) *Attachment*, vol. 1 of *Attachment and loss* (2nd edition 1982), London: Hogarth Press; New York: Basic Books; Harmondsworth: Penguin (1971).

Bowlby, J. (1973) *Separation: anxiety and anger*, vol. 2 of *Attachment and loss*, London: Hogarth Press; New York: Basic Books; Harmondsworth: Penguin (1975).

Bowlby, J. (1977) 'The making and breaking of affectional bonds', *British Journal of Psychiatry*, 130: 201–10 and 421–31; reprinted 1979, New York: Methuen Inc.; London: Tavistock.

Bowlby, J. (1980) *Loss: sadness and depression*, vol. 3 of *Attachment and loss*, London: Hogarth Press; New York: Basic Books; Harmondsworth: Penguin (1981).

Bowlby, J. (1981) 'Psychoanalysis as a natural science', *International Review of Psycho-Analysis*, 8: 243–56.

Bowlby, J. (1982) *Attachment*, 2nd edition of vol. 1 of *Attachment and loss* London: Hogarth Press.

Brazelton, T.B., Koslowski, B., and Main, M. (1974) 'The origins of reciprocity in mother–infant interaction' in M. Lewis and L.A. Rosenblum (eds) *The Effect of the Infant on its Caregiver*, 49–76, New York; Wiley-Interscience.

Bretherton, I. (1987) 'New perspectives on attachment relations in infancy: security, communication and internal working models' in J.D. Osofsky, (ed.) *Handbook of infant development* (2nd edition), 1061–100, New York: Wiley.

Brown, G.W. and Harris, T. (1978) *The social origins of depression*, London: Tavistock.

Burlingham, D. and Freud, A. (1942) *Young children in war-time London*, London: Allen & Unwin.

Burlingham, D. and Freud, A. (1944) *Infants without families*, London: Allen & Unwin.

Burnham, D.L. (1965) 'Separation anxiety', *Archives of General Psychiatry*, 13: 346–58.

Cain, A.C. and Fast, I. (1972) 'Children's disturbed reactions to parent suicide' in A.C. Cain (ed.) *Survivors of suicide*, Springfield, Illinois: C.C. Thomas.

Casement, P. (1985) *On learning from the patient*, London: Tavistock.

Cassidy, J. and Kobak, R. (1988) 'Avoidance and its relation to other defensive processes' in J. Belsky and T. Nezworski (eds.) *Clinical Implications of Attachment*, Hillsdale, NJ: Lawrence Erlbaum.

Cater, J.I. and Easton, P.M. (1980) 'Separation and other stress in child abuse', *Lancet*, 1 (3 May 1980): 972.

Clarke-Stewart, K.A. (1978) 'And daddy makes three: the father's impact on mother and young child', *Child Development*, 49: 466–78.

Collis, G.M. and Schaffer, H.R. (1975) 'Synchronization of visual attention in mother-infant pairs', *Journal of Child Psychology and Psychiatry*, 16: 315–20.

Crittenden, P. (1985) 'Maltreated infants: vulnerability and resilience', *Journal of Child Psychology and Psychiatry* 26: 85–96.

DeLozier, P.P. (1982) 'Attachment theory and child abuse' in C.M. Parkes and J Stevenson-Hinde *The place of attachment in human behavior*, 95–117, New York: Basic Books; London: Tavistock.

Deutsch, H. (1937) 'Absence of grief', *Psychoanalytic Quarterly*, 6: 12–22.

Dixon, N.F. (1971) *Subliminal perception: the nature of a controversy*, London: McGraw-Hill.

Dixon, N.F. (1981) *Preconscious processing*, Chichester and New York: Wiley.

Efron, A. (1977) 'Freud's self-analysis and the nature of psycho-analytic critism', *International Review of Psycho-analysis*, 4: 253–80.

Emde, R.N. (1983) 'The prerepresentational self and its affective core', *The Psychoanalytic Study of the Child*, 38: 165–92.

Epstein, S. (1980) 'The self-concept: a review of the proposal of an integrated theory of personality' in E. Staub (ed.) *Personality: basic issues and current research*, Englewood Cliffs, NJ: Prentice Hall.

Epstein, S. (1986) 'Implications of cognitive self-theory for psychopathology and psychotherapy' in N. Cheshire and H. Thoma (eds) *Self-esteem and Psychotherapy*, New York: Wiley.

Erdelyi, M.H. (1974) 'A new look at the New Look: perceptual defense and vigilance', *Psychological Review*, 81: 1–25.

Fairbairn, W.R.D. (1940) 'Schizoid factors in the personality' in *Psycho-analytic studies of the Personality*, 3–27, London: Tavistock (1952); New York: Basic Books (1952).

Farrington, D.P. (1978) 'The family backgrounds of aggressive youths' in L. Hersov and M. Berger (eds) *Aggression and anti-social behaviour in children and adolescents*, 73–93, Oxford and New York: Pergamon Press.

Feinstein, H.M., Paul, N., and Pettison, E. (1964) 'Group therapy for mothers with infanticidal impulses', *American Journal of Psychiatry*, 120: 882–6.

Fraiberg, S., Adelson, E., and Shapiro, V. (1975) 'Ghosts in the nursery: a psychoanalytic approach to the problems of impaired infant–mother relationships', *Journal of the American Academy of Child Psychiatry*, 14: 387–421.

Freud, S. (1909) 'Analysis of a phobia in a five-year-old boy', *Standard Edition 10*, 5–149, London: Hogarth Press.

Freud, S. (1914) 'Remembering, repeating and working through', *SE* 12, 147–56, London: Hogarth Press.

Freud, S. (1917) *Introductory lectures on psycho-analysis Part III*, *SE* 16, 243–476, London: Hogarth Press.

Freud, S. (1918) 'From the history of an infantile neurosis', *SE* 17, 7–122, London: Hogarth Press.

Freud, S. (1925) 'An autobiographical study', *SE* 20, 7–70, London: Hogarth Press.

Freud, S. (1926) *Inhibitions, symptoms and anxiety*, *SE* 20, 87–174, London: Hogarth Press.

Freud, S. (1937) 'Constructions in analysis', *SE* 23, 257–69, London: Hogarth Press.

Freud, S. (1939) 'Moses and monotheism', *SE* 23, 7–137, London: Hogarth Press.

Freud, S. (1940) 'An outline of psycho-analysis', *SE* 23, 144–207, London: Hogarth Press.

Freud, S. (1950) 'Project for a scientific psychology', *SE1*, 295–397, London: Hogarth Press.

Frodi, A.M. and Lamb, M.E. (1980) 'Child abusers' responses to infant smiles and cries', *Child Development*, 51: 238–41.

Frommer, E.A. and O'Shea, G. (1973) 'Antenatal identification of women liable to have problems in managing their infants', *British Journal of Psychiatry*, 123, 149–56.

Furman, E. (1974) *A child's parent dies*, New Haven and London: Yale University Press.

Gaensbauer, T.J. and Sands, K. (1979) 'Distorted affective communications in abused/neglected infants and their potential impact on caretakers', *Journal of the American Academy of Child Psychiatry*, 18: 236–50.

Gayford, J.J. (1975) 'Wife-battering; a preliminary survey of 100 cases',

British Medical Journal, vol. 1, 194–7, no. 5951.

Gedo, J.E. (1979) *Beyond interpretation: toward a revised theory for psychoanalysis*, New York: International Universities Press.

George, C. and Main, M. (1979) 'Social interactions of young abused children: approach, avoidance and aggression', *Child Development*, 50: 306–18.

Gill, H.S. (1970) 'Parental influences in a child's capacity to perceive sexual themes', *Family Process* 9: 41–50; reprinted in R. Gosling (ed.) *Support, innovation and autonomy*, 113–24, London: Tavistock (1973).

Goldfarb, W. (1943a) 'Infant rearing and problem behaviour', *American Journal of Orthopsychiatry*, 13: 249–65.

Goldfarb, W. (1943b) 'The effect of early institutional care on adolescent personality', *Child Development*, 14: 213–23.

Goldfarb, W. (1943c) 'The effects of early institutional care on adolescent personality', *Journal of Experimental Education*, 12: 106–29.

Goldfarb, W. (1955) 'Emotional and intellectual consequences of psychologic deprivation in infancy: a revaluation' in P.H. Hoch and J. Zubin (eds) *Psychopathology of Childhood*, New York: Grune & Stratton.

Green, A.H., Gaines, R.W., and Sandgrun, A. (1974) 'Child abuse: pathological syndrome of family interaction', *American Journal of Psychiatry*, 131, 882–6.

Grinker, R.R. (1962) '"Mentally healthy" young males (homoclites)', *Archives of General Psychiatry*, 6: 405–53.

Grossmann, K.E., Grossmann, K., and Schwan, A. (1986) 'Capturing the wider view of attachment: a reanalysis of Ainsworth's strange situation' in C.E. Izard and P.B. Read (eds.) *Measuring emotions in infants and children*, vol. 2, New York: Cambridge University Press.

Guidano, V.F. and Liotti, G. (1983) *Cognitive processes and emotional disorders*, New York: Guilford Press.

Guntrip, H. (1975) 'My experience of analysis with Fairbairn and Winnicott', *International Review of Psycho-Analysis*, 2: 145–56.

Hall, F., Pawlby, S.J. and Wolkind, S. (1979) 'Early life experiences and later mothering behaviour: a study of mothers and their 20-week old babies' in D. Shaffer and J. Dunn (eds) *The first year of life*, 153–74, Chichester and New York: Wiley.

Hansburg, H.G. (1972) *Adolescent separation anxiety: a method for the study of adolescent separation problems*, Springfield, Illinois: C.C. Thomas.

Harlow, H.F. and Harlow, M.K. (1965) 'The affectional systems' in A.M. Schrier, H.F. Harlow, and F. Stollnitz (eds) *Behaviour of non-human primates*, vol, 2, New York and London: Academic Press.

Harlow, H.F. and Zimmermann, R.R. (1959) 'Affectional responses in the infant monkey', *Science*, 130: 421.

Harris, T.O. (in press) 'Psycho-social vulnerability to depression: the biographical perspective of the Bedford College studies' in S. Henderson (ed.) *Textbook of Social Psychiatry*, Amsterdam: Elsevier.

Harrison, M. (1981) 'Home-start: a voluntary home-visiting scheme for young families', *Child Abuse and Neglect*, 5: 441–7.

Hazan, C. and Shaver, P. (1987) 'Romantic love conceptualised as an attachment process', *Journal of Personality and Social Psychology*, 52: 511–24.

Heinicke, C. (1956) 'Some effects of separating two-year-old children from their parents: a comparative study', *Human Relations*, 9: 105–76.

Heinicke, C. and Westheimer, I. (1966) *Brief separations*, New York: International Universities Press; London: Longman.

Helfer, R.E. and Kempe, C.H. (eds) (1976) *Child abuse and neglect: the family and the community*, Cambridge, Mass.: Ballinger.

Hinde, R.A. (1974) *Biological bases of human social behaviour*, New York and London: McGraw-Hill.

Hinde, R.A., and Spencer-Booth, Y. (1971) 'Effects of brief separation from mother on rhesus monkeys', *Science*, 173: 111–18.

Hinde, R.A., Perret-Clermont, A.-N., and Stevenson-Hinde J. (eds) (1985) *Social relationships and cognitive development*, Oxford: Clarendon Press.

Holt, R.R. (1981) 'The death and transfiguration of metapsychology', *International Review of Psycho-Analysis*, 8: 129–43.

Home, H.J. (1966) 'The concept of mind', *International Journal of Psycho-Analysis*, 47: 43–9.

Hopkins, J. (1984) 'The probable role of trauma in a case of foot and shoe fetishism: aspects of the psychotherapy of a six-year-old girl', *International Review of Psycho-analysis*, 11: 79–91.

Horney, K. (1951) *Neurosis and human growth*, London: Routledge & Kegan Paul.

Horowitz, M., Marmar, C., Krupnick, J., Wilner, N., Kaltreider N., and Wallerstein, R. (1984) *Personality styles and brief psychotherapy*, New York: Basic Books.

Izard, C.E. (ed.) (1982) *Measuring emotions in infants and children*, Cambridge: Cambridge University Press.

Johnson-Laird, P.N. (1983) *Mental models*, Cambridge: Cambridge University Press.

Jones, E. (1957) *Sigmund Freud: life and work*, vol. 3, London: Hogarth Press, New York: Basic Books.

Kaye, H. (1977) 'Infant sucking behaviour and its modification' in L.P.

Lipsitt and C.C. Spiker (eds) *Advances in child development and behaviour*, vol. 3, 2–52, London and New York: Academic Press.

Kennell, J.H., Jerrauld, R., Wolfe, H., Chesler, D., Kreger, N.C., McAlpine, W., Steffa, M., and Klaus, M.H. (1974) 'Maternal behaviour one year after early and extended post-partum contact', *Developmental Medicine and Child Neurology*, 16: 172–9.

Kernberg, O. (1975) *Borderline conditions and pathological narcissism*, New York: Jason Aronson.

Kernberg, O. (1980) *Internal world and external reality: object relations theory applied*, New York: Jason Aronson.

Klaus, M.H. and Kennell, J.H. (1982) *Maternal–infant bonding* (2nd edition), St Louis: C.V. Mosby.

Klaus, M.H., Trause, M.A., and Kennell, J.H. (1975) 'Does human maternal behaviour after delivery show a characteristic pattern?' in *Parent-infant interaction, Ciba Foundation Symposium 33 (new series)*: 69–78, Amsterdam: Elsevier.

Klaus, M.H., Kennell, J.H., Robertson, S.S., and Sosa, R. (1986) 'Effects of social support during parturition on maternal and infant morbidity', *British Medical Journal*, 283: 585–7.

Klein, G.S. (1976) *Psychoanalytic theory: an exploration of essentials*, New York: International Universities Press.

Klein, M. (1940) 'Mourning and its relation to manic-depressive states' in *Love, guilt and reparation and other papers, 1921–1946*, 311–38, London: Hogarth (1947); Boston: Seymour Lawrence/Delacorte.

Klein, Milton (1981) 'On Mahler's autistic and symbiotic phases: an exposition and evaluation', *Psychoanalysis and Contemporary Thought*, 4: 69–105.

Kliman, G. (1965) *Psychological emergencies of childhood*, New York: Grune & Stratton.

Kluft, R.P. (ed.) (1985) *Childhood antecedents of multiple personality*, Washington D.C.: American Psychiatric Press.

Kobak, R.R. and Sceery, A. (1988) 'Attachment in late adolescence; working models, affect regulation and representations of self and others'. *Child Development*, 59.

Kohut, H. (1971) *The analysis of the self*, New York: International Universities Press.

Kohut, H. (1977) *The restoration of the self*, New York: International Universities Press.

Kuhn, T.S. (1962) *The structure of scientific revolutions* (2nd edition 1970) Chicago: University of Chicago Press.

Kuhn, T.S. (1974) 'Second thoughts on paradigms' in F. Suppe (ed.) *The structure of scientific theory*, 459–99, Urbana, Illinois: University of Illinois Press.

Lamb, M.E. (1977) 'The development of mother–infant and father–infant attachment in the second year of life', *Developmental Psychology*, 13: 637–48.

Latakos, I. (1974) 'Falsification and the methodology of scientific research programmes' in I. Latakos and A. Musgrave (eds) *Criticism and the growth of knowledge*, London: Cambridge University Press.

Levy, D. (1937) 'Primary affect hunger', *American Journal of Psychiatry*, 94: 643–52.

Lind, E. (1973) 'From false-self to true-self functioning: a case in brief psychotherapy', *British Journal of Medical Psychology*, 46: 381–9.

Liotti, G. (1986) 'Structural cognitive therapy' in W. Dryden and W. Golden (eds.) *Cognitive-behavioural approaches to psychotherapy*, 92–128, New York; Harper & Row.

Liotti, G. (1987) 'The resistance to change of cognitive structures: a counterproposal to psychoanalytic metapsychology', *Journal of Cognitive Psychotherapy*, 1: 87–104.

Lorenz, K.Z. (1935) 'Der Kumpan in der Umvelt des Vogels', *J. Orn. Berl.*, 83, English translation in C.H. Schiller (ed.) *Instinctive behaviour*, New York: International Universities Press (1957).

Lynch, M. (1975) 'Ill-health and child abuse', *The lancet*, 16 August 1975.

Lynch, M.A. and Roberts, J. (1982) *Consequences of child abuse*, London: Academic Press.

Mackey, W.C. (1979) 'Parameters of the adult-male-child bond', *Ethology and Sociobiology* 1: 59–76.

Mahler, M.S. (1971) 'A study of the separation-individuation process and its possible application to borderline phenomena in the psychoanalytic situation', *The psychoanalytic study of the child*, 26: 403–24.

Mahler, M.S., Pine, F., and Bergman, A. (1975) *The psychological birth of the human infant*, New York: Basic Books.

Main, M.B. (1977) 'Analysis of a peculiar form of reunion behaviour in some day-care children: its history and sequelae in children who are home-reared', in R. Webb (ed.) *Social development in childhood: day-care programs and research*, Baltimore: John Hopkins University Press.

Main, M. (1988) 'Parental aversion to physical contact with the infant: stability, consequences and reasons' in T.B. Brazelton and K. Barnard (eds) *Touch* New York: International Universities Press.

Main, M. and Cassidy, J. (1988) 'Categories of response with the parent at age six: predicted from infant attachment classifications and stable over a one month period', *Developmental Psychology*, 24: 415–26.

References

Main, M. and George, C. (1985) 'Responses of abused and disadvantaged toddlers to distress in age-mates: a study in the day-care setting', *Developmental Psychology*, 21, 407–12.

Main, M. and Hesse, E. (in press) 'Lack of resolution of mourning in adulthood and its relationship to infant organization: some speculations regarding causal mechanisms', in M. Greenberg, D. Cicchetti and M. Cummings (eds) *Attachment in the preschool years*, Chicago: University of Chicago Press.

Main, M. and Solomon, J. (in press) 'Procedure for identifying infants as disorganized/disoriented during the Ainsworth Strange Situation' in M. Greenberg, D. Cicchetti, and M. Cummings (eds), *Attachment in the preschool years*, Chicago: University of Chicago Press.

Main, M. and Weston, D. (1981) 'Quality of attachment to mother and to father: related to conflict behaviour and the readiness for establishing new relationships', *Child Development*, 52: 932–940.

Main, M., Kaplan, N., and Cassidy, J. (1985) 'Security in infancy, childhood and adulthood: a move to the level of representation' in I. Bretherton and E. Waters (eds) *Growing points in attachment: theory and research*, Monographs of the Society for Research in Child Development Serial 209: 66–104, Chicago: University of Chicago Press.

Malan, D.M. (1973) 'Therapeutic factors in analytically-oriented brief psychotherapy' in: R.H. Gosling (ed.) *Support, Innovation and Autonomy*, 187–209, London: Tavistock.

Malone, C.A. (1966) 'Safety first: comments on the influence of external danger in the lives of children of disorganized families', *American Journal of Orthopsychiatry* 36: 6–12.

Manning, M., Heron, J., and Marshall, T. (1978) 'Styles of hostility and social interactions at nursery, at school and at home: an extended study of children' in L. Hersov and M. Berger (eds) *Aggression and antisocial behaviour in childhood and adolescence*, 29–58, Oxford and New York: Pergamon.

Marris, P. (1958) *Widows and their families*, London: Routledge & Kegan Paul.

Marrone, M. (1984) 'Aspects of transference in group analysis', *Group Analysis*, 17: 179–90.

Marsden, D. and Owens, D. (1975) 'The Jekyll and Hyde marriages', *New Society*, 32: 333–5.

Martin, H.P. and Rodeheffer, M.A. (1980) 'The psychological impact of abuse in children' in G.J. Williams and J. Money (eds.) *Traumatic abuse and neglect of children at home*, Baltimore, Maryland: Johns Hopkins University Press.

Matas, L., Arend, R.A., and Sroufe, L.A. (1978) 'Continuity of adaptation in the second year: the relationship between quality of attachment and later competence', *Child Development*, 49: 547–56.

Mattinson, J. and Sinclair, I. (1979) *Mate and stalemate*, Oxford:
Blackwell.

Meiselman, K.C. (1978) *Incest – a psychological study of causes and effects
with treatment recommendations*, San Francisco: Jossey-Bass.

Melges, F.T. and DeMaso, D.R. (1980) 'Grief resolution therapy: reliv-
ing, revising, and revisiting', *American Journal of Psychotherapy*, 34:
51–61.

Miller, A. (1979, English translation 1983) *The drama of the gifted child and
the search for the true self*, London: Faber and Faber.

Mintz, T. (1976) 'Contribution to panel report on effects on adults of
object loss in the first five years', reported by M. Wolfenstein,
Journal of the American Psychoanalytic Association, 24, 662–5.

Mitchell, M.C. (in preparation) 'Physical child abuse in a Mexican-
American population' in K.E. Pottharst (ed.) *Research explorations in
adult attachment*.

Morris, D. (1981) 'Attachment and intimacy' in G. Stricker (ed.) *Intimacy*,
New York: Plenum.

Morris, M.G. and Gould, R.W. (1963) 'Role reversal: a necessary concept in dealing with the "Battered child syndrome"', *American Journal
of Orthopsychiatry*, 32: 298–9.

Newson, J. (1977) 'An intersubjective approach to the systematic description of mother–infant interaction', in H.R. Schaffer (ed.) *Studies
in mother–infant interaction*, New York: Academic Press.

Niederland, W.G. (1959a) 'The "miracled-up" world of Schreber's
childhood', *The Psychoanalytic Study of the Child*, 14: 383–413.

Niederland, W.G. (1959b) 'Schreber: father and son', *Psycho–Analytic
Quarterly*, 28: 151–69.

Norman, D.A. (1976) *Memory and attention: introduction to human information processing* (2nd edition), New York: Wiley.

Offer, D. (1969) *The psychological world of the teenager: a study of normal
adolescent boys*, New York: Basic Books.

Palgi, P. (1973) 'The socio-cultural expressions and implications of
death, mourning and bereavement arising out of the war situation
in Israel' *Israel Annals of Psychiatry*, 11: 301–29.

Parke, R.D. (1979) 'Perspectives on father–infant interaction' in J.D.
Osofsky (ed.) *Handbook of infant development*, New York: Wiley.

Parke, R.D. and Collmer, C.W. (1975) 'Child abuse: an interdisciplinary
analysis' in E.M. Hetherington (ed.) *Review of Child Development
Research*, vol. 5, Chicago: University of Chicago Press.

Parkes, C.M. (1972) *Bereavement: studies of grief in adult life*, London: Tavistock; New York: International Universities Press.

Parkes, C.M. and Stevenson-Hinde, J. (eds) (1982) *The place of attachment in human behavior*, New York: Basic Books; London: Tavistock.

Pedder, J. (1976) 'Attachment and new beginning', *International Review of Psycho-analysis*, 3: 491–7.

Peterfreund, E. (1971) *Information, systems, and psychoanalysis*, Psychological Issues, vol.VII. Monograph 25/26, New York: International Universities Press.

Peterfreund, E. (1978) 'Some critical comments on psychoanalytic conceptualizations of infancy', *International Journal of Psycho-Analysis*, 59: 427–41.

Peterfreund, E. (1983) *The process of psychoanalytic therapy: modes and strategies*, New York: Analytic Press.

Peterson, G.H. and Mehl, L.E. (1978) 'Some determinants of maternal attachment', *American Journal of Psychiatry*, 135: 1168–73.

Pine, F. (1985) *Developmental theory and clinical process*, New Haven: Yale University Press.

Popper, K.R. (1972) *Objective knowledge: an evolutionary approach*, Oxford: Clarendon Press.

Pound, A. (1982) 'Attachment and maternal depression' in C.M. Parkes and J. Stevenson-Hinde (eds.) *The place of attachment in human behavior*, 118–130, New York: Basic Books; London: Tavistock.

Pound, A. and Mills, M. (1985) 'A pilot evaluation of Newpin, a home visiting and befriending scheme in South London', *Newsletter of Association for Child Psychology and Psychiatry*, 7, no 4: 13–15.

Provence, S. and Lipton, R.C. (1962) *Infants in institutions*, New York: International Universities Press.

Radford, M. (1983) 'Psychoanalysis and the science of problem-solving man: an application of Popper's philosophy and a response to Will (1980)', *British Journal of Medical Psychology*, 56: 9–26.

Radke-Yarrow, M., Cummings, E.M., Kuczynski, L., and Chapman, M. (1985) 'Patterns of attachment in two- and three-year olds in normal families and families with parental depression', *Child Development*, 56: 884–93.

Rajecki, D.W., Lamb, M.E., and Obmascher, P. (1978) 'Towards a general theory of infantile attachment: a comparative review of aspects of the social bond', *The Behavioral and Brain Sciences*, 3: 417–64.

Raphael, B. (1977) 'Preventive intervention with the recently bereaved', *Archives of General Psychiatry*, 34: 1450–4.

Raphael, B. (1982) 'The young child and the death of a parent' in C.M. Parkes and J. Stevenson-Hinde (eds) *The place of attachment in human behaviour*, 131–50, New York: Basic Books; London: Tavistock.

Raphael, D. (1966) 'The lactation-suckling process within a matrix of supportive behaviour', dissertation for the degree of PhD submitted to Columbia University.

Ricks, M.H. (1985) 'The social transmission of parental behaviour: attachment across generations' in I. Bretherton and E. Waters (eds) *Growing points in attachment theory and research*, Monograph of the Society for Research in Child Development Serial no. 209, 211–27.

Ricoeur, P. (1970) *Freud and philosophy: an essay in interpretation* (trans: D. Savage), New Haven: Yale University Press.

Ringler, N., Kennell, J.H., Jarvella, R., Navajosky, R.J., and Klaus, M.H. (1975) 'Mother to child speech at two years: the effects of increased postnatal contact', *Journal of Pediatrics*, 86, 141–4.

Robertson, J. (1952) *A two year-old goes to hospital* (film), Ipswich: Concord Films Council; New York: New York University Film Library.

Robertson, J. (1953) 'Some responses of young children to loss of maternal care', *Nursing Times*, 49: 382–6.

Robertson, J. (1958) *Going to hospital with mother* (film) Ipswich: Concord Films Council; New York: New York University Film Library.

Robertson, J. (1970) *Young children in hospital* (2nd edition) London: Tavistock.

Robertson, J. and Bowlby, J. (1952) 'Responses of young children to separation from their mothers', *Courrier Centre Internationale Enfance*, 2: 131–42.

Robson, K.M. and Kumar, R. (1980) 'Delayed onset of maternal affection after childbirth', *British Journal of Psychiatry*, 136: 347–53.

Rosen, V.H. (1955) 'The reconstruction of a traumatic childhood event in a case of derealization', *Journal of the American Psychoanalytic Association*, 3: 211–21; reprinted in A.C. Cain (ed.) (1972) *Survivors of suicide*, Springfield, Illinois: C.C. Thomas.

Rosenblatt, A.D. and Thickstun, J.T. (1977) *Modern psychoanalytic concepts in a general psychology*, parts 1 and 2, Psychological Issues Monograph 42/43, New York: International Universities Press.

Rosenfeld, S. (1975) 'Some reflections arising from the treatment of a traumatized child' in *Hampstead Clinic Studies in Child Psychoanalysis*, 47–64, New Haven, Conn.: Yale University Press.

Rubinstein, B.B. (1967) 'Explanation and mere description: a meta-scientific examination of certain aspects of the psychoanalytic theory of motivation' in R.R. Holt (ed.) *Motives and thought: psychoanalytic essays in honor of David Rapaport*, 20–7, Psychological Issues Monograph 18/19, New York: International Universities Press.

Rutter, M. (1979) 'Maternal deprivation, 1972–1978: new findings, new concepts, new approaches', *Child Development*, 50: 283–305; reprinted in *Maternal Deprivation Reassessed* (2nd edition), Harmondsworth: Penguin, 1981.

Rutter, M. (ed.) (1980) *Scientific foundation of developmental psychiatry*, London: Heinemann Medical Books.

Sameroff, A.J. and Chandler, M.A. (1975) 'Reproductive risk and the continuance of caretaking casualty' in F.D. Horowitz, *et al.* (eds) *Review of Child Development Research*, vol.4, 187–244, Chicago: University of Chicago Press.

Sander, L.W. (1964) 'Adaptive relationships in early mother–child interaction', *Journal of the American Academy of Child Psychiatry*, 3: 231–64.

Sander, L.W. (1977) 'The regulation of exchange in the infant-caregiver system and some aspects of the context–content relationships' in M. Lewis and L. Rosenblum (eds) *Interaction, conversation and the development of language*, 133–56, New York and London: Wiley.

Sander, L. (reporter) (1980) 'New knowledge about the infant from current research: implications for psychoanalysis', Report of panel held at the Annual Meeting of the American Psychoanalytic Association, Atlanta, May 1978, *Journal of the American Psychoanalytic Association*, 28: 181–98.

Santayana, G. (1905) *The life of reason*, vol.1, New York: Scribner.

Schafer, R. (1976) *A new language for psychoanalysis*, New Haven: Yale University Press.

Schaffer, H.R. (ed.) (1977) *Studies in mother–infant interaction*, London: Academic Press.

Schaffer, H.R. (1979) 'Acquiring the concept of the dialogue' in H.M. Bornstein and W. Kessen (eds) *Psychological development from infancy: image to intention*, 279–305, Hillsdale, New Jersey: Lawrence Erlbaum.

Schaffer, H.R. and Crook, C.K. (1979) 'The role of the mother in early social development' in B. McGurk (ed.) *Issues in childhood social development*, 55–78, London: Methuen.

Schaffer, H.R., Collis, G.M., and Parsons, G. (1977) 'Vocal interchange and visual regard in verbal and preverbal children', in H.R. Schaffer (ed.) *Studies in mother–infant interaction*, 291–324, London: Academic Press.

Sosa, R., Kennell, J., Klaus, M., Robertson, S., and Urrutia, J. (1980) 'The effect of a supportive companion on length of labour, mother–infant interaction and perinatal problems', *New England Journal of Medicine*, 303: 597–600.

171

Spiegel, R. (1981) 'Review of *Loss: Sadness and Depression* by John Bowlby', *American Journal of Psychotherapy*, 35: 598–600.

Spinetta, J.J. and Rigler, D. (1972) 'The child-abusing parent: a psychological review', *Psychological Bulletin*, 77: 296–304.

Spitz, R.A. (1945) 'Hospitalism: an enquiry into the genesis of psychiatric conditions in early childhood', *The Psychoanalytic Study of the Child*, 1: 53–74.

Spitz, R.A. (1946) 'Anaclitic depression', *The Psychoanalytic Study of the Child*, 2: 313–42.

Spitz, R.A. (1947) *Grief: a peril in infancy* (film), New York: New York University Film Library.

Spitz, R.A. (1957) *No and yes*, New York: International Universities Press.

Sroufe, L.A. (1983) 'Infant–caregiver attachment and patterns of adaptation in pre-school: the roots of maladaptation and competence', in M. Perlmutter (ed.) *Minnesota Symposium in Child Psychology, vol. 16*, 41–81, Minneapolis: University of Minnesota Press.

Sroufe, L.A. (1985) 'Attachment-classification from the perspective of infant–caregiver relationships and infant temperament', *Child Development*, 56: 1–14.

Sroufe, L.A. (1986) 'Bowlby's contribution to psychoanalytic theory and developmental psychology', *Journal of Child Psychology and Psychiatry*, 27: 841–9.

Steele, B.F. and Pollock, C.B. (1968) 'A psychiatric study of parents who abuse infants and small children' in R.E. Helfer and C.H. Kempe (eds) *The battered child*, 103–45, Chicago: University of Chicago Press.

Stephen, A. (1934) 'On defining psychoanalysis', *British Journal of Medical Psychology*, 11: 101–16.

Stern, D.N. (1977) *The first relationship: infant and mother*, London: Fontana, Open Books.

Stern, D.N. (1985) *The interpersonal world of the infant*, New York: Basic Books.

Strachey, J. (1959), Editor's introduction to the *Standard Edition* of Freud's *Inhibitions, Symptoms and Anxiety*, SE 20, 77–86, London: Hogarth Press.

Stroh, G. (1974) 'Psychotic children' in P. Barker (ed.) *The residential psychiatric treatment of children*, 175–90, London: Crosby.

Strupp, H.H. and Binder, J.L. (1984) *Psychotherapy in a new key: a guide to time-limited dynamic psychotherapy*, New York: Basic Books.

Sulloway, F. (1979) *Freud, biologist of the mind*, New York: Basic Books.

Svejda, M.J., Campos, J.J., and Emde, R.N. (1980) 'Mother–infant bonding: failure to generalize', *Child Development*, 51: 775–9.

Trevarthen, C. (1979) 'Instincts for human understanding and for cultural co-operation: their development in infancy', in M. von Cranach, K. Foppa, W. Lepenies, and D. Ploog (eds) *Human Ethology*, 539–71, Cambridge: Cambridge University Press.

van der Eyken, W. (1982) *Home-start: a four-year evaluation*, Leicester: Home-Start Consultancy (140 New Walk, Leicester LE1 7JL).

Waddington, C.H. (1957) *The strategy of the genes*, London: Allen & Unwin.

Wärtner, U.G. (1986) 'Attachment in infancy and at age six, and children's self-concept: a follow-up of a German longitudinal study', doctoral dissertation, University of Virginia.

Weisskopf, V.F. (1981) 'The frontiers and limits of physical sciences' *Bulletin of the American Academy of Arts and Sciences*, 34.

Wenner, N.K. (1966) 'Dependency patterns in pregnancy', in J.H. Masserman (ed.) *Sexuality of women*, 94–104, New York: Grune & Stratton.

Winnicott, C. (1980) 'Fear of breakdown: a clinical example', *International Journal of Psycho-Analysis*, 61: 351–7.

Winnicott, D.W. (1957) 'Primary maternal preoccupation', in *Collected papers: through paediatrics to psychoanalysis*, 300–5, London: Tavistock.

Winnicott, D.W. (1960) 'Ego distortion in terms of true and false self', reprinted in D.W. Winnicott (1965) *The maturational process and the facilitating environment*, 140–52, London: Hogarth; New York: International Universities Press.

Winnicott, D. (1974) 'Fear of breakdown', *International Review of Psycho-analysis*, 1: 103–7.

Wolkind, S., Hall, F., and Pawlby, S. (1977) 'Individual differences in mothering behaviour: a combined epidemiological and observational approach' in P.J. Graham (ed.) *Epidemiological approaches in child psychiatry*, 107–23, New York: Academic Press.

Zahn-Waxler, C., Radke-Yarrow, M., and King, R.A. (1979) 'Child-rearing and children's prosocial initiations toward victims of distress', *Child Development*, 50: 319–30.

Appendix to references

Child made family scapegoat

Gillett, R. (1986) 'Short-term intensive psychotherapy – a case history', *British Journal of Psychiatry*, 148: 98–100.

Parent uses guilt-inducing techniques

Griffin, P. (1986) *Along with youth: Hemingway, the early years*, Oxford: Oxford University Press.

Child target of physical abuse

(a) Developmental studies

Crittenden, P. (1985) 'Maltreated infants: vulnerability and resilience', *Journal of Child Psychology and Psychiatry*, 26: 85–96.

George, C. and Main, M. (1979) 'Social interactions of young abused children: approach, avoidance and aggression', *Child Development*, 50: 306–18.

Main, M. and George, C. (1985) 'Responses of abused and disadvantaged toddlers to distress in age mates: a study in the day-care setting', *Developmental Psychology*, 21: 407–12.

(b) Therapeutic studies

Hopkins, J. (1984) 'The probable role of trauma in a case of foot and shoe fetishism: aspects of the psychotherapy of a 6-year-old girl', *International Review of Psychoanalysis*, 11: 79–91.

Hopkins, J. (1986) 'Solving the mystery of monsters: steps towards the recovery from trauma', *Journal of Child Psychotherapy*, 12: 61–71.

Lanyado, M. (1985) 'Surviving trauma: dilemmas in the psychotherapy of traumatised children', *British Journal of Psychotherapy*, 2: 50–62.

Child target of sexual abuse

Bass, E. and Thornton, L. (eds) (1983) *I never told anyone: writings by women survivors of child sexual abuse*, New York: Harper & Row.

Herman, J.L. (1981) *Father-daughter incest*, Cambridge, Mass.: Harvard University Press.

Herman, J., Russell, D., and Trocki, K. (1986) 'Longterm effects of incestuous abuse in childhood', *American Journal of Psychiatry*, 143: 1293–6.

Name index

Subject index

abuse, *see* child abuse
adolescents 2, 3, 11, 30, 62, 82, 122
affectional bonds, *see* bonding
aggressive behaviour 16–18, 77–98,
113, 116–17
amnesia 99, 101–16
anger 4, 26, 30–3, 50, 79–81, 108,
145, 155
anxiety 4, 29–31, 49, 85; *see also*
attachment, separation
attachment
theory of 4, 26–8, 61–6, 81–3, 119–
36; patterns of 123–9; history of
theory of 20–38; secure/insecure
10–11, 72–3, 123–6, 128–9, 130–3;
anxious resistant 124, 130–2, 133–4;
anxious avoidant 50–3, 124, 130–2,
133–4, 143; implications of for
therapy 18–19, 37–8, 71–4, 137–57

battering, *see* child abuse
babies, *see* infants
base, *see* secure base
behaviourism 28
bereavement, *see* loss *and* mourning
birth, circumstances surrounding
delivery 13–15
bonding 15, 25, 120–3

caregiving and careseeking 2, 81–3,
121–3; *see also* parenting
child abuse 16–18, 37, 83–93, 116–17

childhood experiences, effects of
on parental behaviour 36–7, 43–7,
91–5, 133–5; on child's behaviour
36–7, 43–7
clinging behaviour 33, 124, 126, 135–6
cognitive disorders 99–117
cognitive psychology 34–5
control systems 26, 33–4, 61–3, 120
crying 49, 53, 88, 106–7, 122

Darwinism and neo-Darwinism 66
defensive exclusion 26, 33–5
defensive processes 26, 33–5
denials 32, 102–6, 142–51
dependency 3, 12, 24–7, 54, 62, 84,
88, 119
depression 4, 26, 31, 49, 105, 108
deprivation, *see* maternal deprivation
despair 32, 50, 81
detachment 32, 33–5, 50–1, 70
developmental pathways 26, 64–6,
120, 135–6
dichotic listening experiments 111–
12
discipline 12
disclaimers 102–6, 142, 148–51

emotions, *see* feelings
ethology 1, 3–6, 25–7, 81–3, 120
evolution 81–3, 120
exploratory behaviour 46–8, 61–2,
121–2, 140